This novel is dedicated to those who have believed in my ability as an author and have encouraged me to proceed with my dream.

Fire Rider

ISBN - 978-1-8380209-5-8

Published in 2020

Illustrations by Analdo Arscott

Please visit ***www.paulgaskill.co.uk***
for more details about the author and his books.

Fire Rider

The Oracus Series

Book Number One

Paul Gaskill

Contents

ONE

Attempted Escape

The wind swirled through the leaves of the trees as Catania scampered over the forest floor below. It was the warmest night in memory, and every breath was dry and sharp in her throat. She hadn't been so far north in a long time, not since she had been forced to leave her son and his father, and she had forgotten just how hot the forest could be.

When Catania came to a halt, she could still hear the thundering approach of the King's men through the trees. Their menacing shouts and rattling armour were loud enough to stifle the sound of her thumping heart, and her panic was so intense it hurt. Her senses were sharp – she could feel beads of sweat gathering on her face, taste smoke on the earthy air, and see tiny, glowing insects fluttering from bush to bush. But she was still too weak to outrun the men. She was no longer a Rider, only Human.

She continued to retreat from the danger and made her winding escape through the thickening trees. Her pale skin was cut and scratched as she waded through the dense shrubbery that impeded her path, and the uneven ground caused her to stumble clumsily with every other step.

The moonlight showered her as she tumbled heavily into a small clearing. She fumbled momentarily with the dirt beneath her before staggering to unsteady feet. She stood alone and uncertain, with blonde hair flowing wildly over her beautiful face, and her white linen dress badly ripped and soiled. Only the intimidating silhouettes of the trees and the taunting echoes of her enemy's shouts revealed themselves. Catania knew she must flee, but fear held her in place. She was exhausted, and her chest tremored painfully with every breath she inhaled.

An inevitable slither of orange light appeared from within the trees and Catania knew the end was near. She was surely gasping her last few breaths of life. She whimpered with despair as her incredible life flashed vividly before her eyes – she remembered her time in the two cities she had once called home, the turbulent relationship she had shared with her father, the short time she had spent with her baby son before leaving him, the majestic Lavorians of the land, and the superpowers that those Lavorians gifted their Riders.

Dropping to her knees, Catania accepted defeat as the yelling men and their lights drew nearer. The men were visible now, the flames of their torches licking at their armoured bodies, and their swords unsheathed and ready to cut at her delicate body. These men were soldiers of the King, both vicious and cruel. They approached her with ridiculing smiles on their faces; her terror was their delight.

Catania scurried away from them until her back pressed against the gnarled trunk of a tree. She tried to hold back her sobs, but uncontrollable tears trickled down her cheeks. She was helpless and frightened, and she prayed that her death would be a quick and painless one. But with the way the shadows danced over the demonic faces of the soldiers, she knew it would be slow and agonising instead.

It seemed impossible that anything could save her now, but when a menacing growl was carried into the clearing upon the wind, the soldiers faltered, and Catania's hopes rose. From within the trees, there was a scampering of paws followed by an enraged howl that could make blood curdle. A wonderful silence had swept over the soldiers as they squinted with uncertainty into the darkness around them. They edged closer together, forming a tight group, and they all held their torches aloft and their swords out in front of them.

From out of the trees to Catania's left, a wolf padded delicately into the clearing. It was more than twice the size of an ordinary wolf and its fur was as white as snow. It came to a halt between Catania and her attackers, protecting her from harm.

"Alticon!" Catania whimpered with relief. "You came!"

The wolf's tail twitched in response, but its eyes, which were glimmering with the reflection of the flaming torches, never left the soldiers.

For a short time, Catania thought the sudden appearance of Alticon might force the soldiers to flee. In the past, they would have, but Alticon was no longer a Lavorian, just as Catania was no longer a Rider. He had been stripped of his armour, Catania had been stripped of her powers, and together they had been stripped of their incredible telepathic bond. Had it been the past, the soldiers would already be dead, but Alticon was vulnerable now and the soldiers knew it. Glancing at each other, they found the courage to approach him with their swords still raised.

As they neared, Alticon clawed at the nearest man and dropped him to the ground in a flash. The second soldier succumbed to the same fate. As did the third. But the fourth to confront Alticon swung his fiery torch and sprinkled sparks at the wolf's feet. The embers of the torch set alight the dry forest floor and a wave of heat rose with the flames. Alticon stepped back with a snarl, and the soldiers willingly seized the advantage, pressing through the flames and aiming their blades at the wolf's face and body.

In moments, Alticon's flawless white fur was marked with crimson stains. As he withdrew from the soldiers, he seemed smaller and less fierce. Only six of the men remained, but with the swelling fire aiding them, it was unlikely that Alticon would defeat them. Then inevitably, with the men continuing to bear down on him, he fell with a whine of pain beneath their swords.

Catania jumped to her feet and prepared to defend her rescuer. But without a weapon of her own, she was easily overpowered by one of the soldiers and took a heavy blow to the head. Abruptly, she was on the ground again, now with warm blood oozing from her head and the dark forest spinning around her. Smoke from the fire hampered her breathing and she could hear nothing but crackling flames and the sadistic, triumphant shouts of the soldiers.

In her final moments of consciousness, Catania wished to call out to Alticon and tell him everything would be okay. But her voice failed her. And as her sight focused for the last time, she saw the blade of a sword disappear into the wolf's chest. A defeated howl echoed around the clearing, and then silence fell.

TWO

Thessley Village

Oracus sat in the corner of his bedroom with a sword in one hand and a whetstone in the other. It was mid-morning, and bright sunlight shone through the open window and bounced off the sword's silver blade. There was a loud ring with each rub of stone on metal, and the sword would vibrate in Oracus's hand, while the green emerald forged into the hilt appeared to glow brighter with every touch on the blade. The sword had belonged to Oracus's father, but had been passed to Oracus when he first started sword practise with the village trainer a year or so ago. Since then, he had kept the sword pristine; both polishing and sharpening it almost every day.

When Oracus was satisfied with how the sword looked and felt, he placed it on the bed and rose. He stood still for a moment and listened to the gentle hum of bees in the flowers outside his window and the soft creak of his father's rocking chair coming from beyond his bedroom door. Then he turned to face the room and swept his blonde hair out of his face. He was nineteen years old, with green eyes that matched the emerald in the hilt of his sword and skin as smooth as glass. He was tall and slim, but with toned muscles from all his time spent hunting in the forest and hammering at the blacksmith's forge. Today he was wearing his training clothes in readiness for sword practise; a black leather gilet over a white shirt, black shorts, and his lightest pair of leather boots. The air in the village was often hot and dry at this time of year, so he wanted to be as cool and comfortable as possible during what he expected to be a very gruelling morning of training.

Returning to his bed, Oracus grabbed his sword from upon it and pulled the sheet and blanket neatly into place. He propped the sword against the foot of the bed along with a wooden shield and several other swords he had crafted at the blacksmith's workshop, and then moved his birch bow and quiver of arrows away from the sharp blades and leaned them gently in the corner.

Above the bed was an untidy collection of books on a shelf which Oracus read during the long hours at night when he couldn't sleep. He would regularly read by lamplight under the covers of his bed, or scan the drawings on the pages. Some of the books were guides or manuals to help him with sword-making, hunting, farming, and so forth. But his favourites were the myths and fairytales. In particular, *The Beasts of Legend*, the tallest, thinnest book on the shelf. With his focus upon it, he pulled the book free of the others and eagerly flicked through the pages, of which each one had a drawing of a terrifying creature. But on the very last page, where a beast of legend should have been drawn, there was only a large question-mark and a small block of text.

Oracus smiled and read the words:

The Bandor

There is talk of a creature of such depravity that it strikes fear into the heart of all mankind. The Bandor.

Silent and undetectable, the Bandor only ever reveals itself when its teeth are clamped securely around its victim's throat.

This creature's appearance is unknown; there have been no recorded sightings. Over hundreds of years, thousands of men have died attempting to discover this beast. Its inconceivable deception makes it difficult to find and impossible to capture.

The Bandor is the predator of all predators, so if you are unfortunate enough to encounter it, then may you rest in peace.

With another smile, Oracus closed the book and slotted it neatly back on the shelf. Then he left the bedroom and proceeded to the sitting room, where his father was still rocking in his chair, pipe in hand and blowing rings of smoke towards the ceiling. Oracus was of the same height and build as his father, but his father had dark hair and a beard. His skin was well-worn too, unlike Oracus's, but his eyes were the same dazzling green.

"Morning, son," he uttered calmly between exhales of smoke. "Are you training today?"

"Morning," Oracus replied. "I'll be leaving as soon as

I've eaten." He walked through to the kitchen and poured some oats into a bowl. Then he returned to the sitting room and began to eat. "And I'm meeting Garrin at the inn tonight too. We're having a drink together before he leaves tomorrow."

Garrin was Oracus's best friend and had been since they were children. Recently, Garrin had become a tradesman, one of only a handful of men to ever travel beyond the village border. And whenever he returned home, Oracus would always question him about the land outside, but Garrin was never willing to answer. It was a village law that tradesmen must keep their dealings private; neither talk of the village to outsiders, nor talk of outsiders to the village.

"Leaving Thessley again already, eh?" Oracus's father sighed. "How long for this time?"

"A month he says. But what could he possibly be trading that will mean he can't return for a whole month?"

Oracus's father shrugged, "That's not for us to know, son."

The truth was that Oracus was desperate to know, and he intended to quiz Garrin about it again when they met at the inn in the evening. All Oracus knew was that Thessley was surrounded by the Raspian Forest, and it sat somewhere to the north of the land, known as Pharia. And even *that* was knowing too much, apparently.

When he had finished eating, Oracus grabbed his sword and shield from his bedroom and left for the village centre, where sword practise was always held. Outside the house, a dozen identical thatched houses lined the street. One way, the street opened wide and meandered towards the village centre. In the other direction, trees of the Raspian Forest stood patient and foreboding.

Oracus took the path away from the forest and walked beneath blue sky and a scorching summer sun whilst listening to the tranquil calls of the birds above. He thought only of the forest's calming aroma mixed with the stench of the farm before he reached the centre of the village, and then a rumble of noise washed over him. Suddenly, villagers were everywhere and all things peaceful were pushed from his mind.

The village centre was a circular plaza of shops and stalls with a fenced training area in the middle. There was a carpentry workshop, a village hall, a clothing stall, and the blacksmith's workshop where Oracus worked. There was also a grocery stall with an abundance of root vegetables and ripe fruits, a jewellery stall with gold and silver chains and gems of a thousand different colours, and a florist's stall with many pots full of shrubs and flowers. Across from Oracus was the entrance to the farmyard which Oracus's father owned and used to breed livestock, and beside it was a butcher's shop with pheasants and rabbits hanging in the window. Outside the butcher's shop, a porky man named Broid stood watchfully, wearing an apron covered in blood. Then lastly to catch Oracus's eye was the Old Mill Inn, with its blockwork covered from top to bottom in dark green ivy.

With both sword and shield in hand, Oracus approached the training area to where a small crowd of men and women of varying ages were waiting to start practise. Oracus could see that all the usual villagers had turned up, and there were no new faces. Except one – Garrin.

"Surprise!" Garrin proclaimed as he saw Oracus walking towards him.

"What are you doing here?" Oracus responded.

"It's my last day before I set off travelling so I thought I'd come and have some fun." He offered Oracus a toothy grin.

When Oracus and Garrin had been young children, many of the villagers had mistaken them for brothers. They had always looked similar and spent so much time together causing mischief on the farm that it would have been odd for people to have thought any different. They shared the same blonde hair, shape of face, and smile, but Garrin was slightly taller than Oracus, and Oracus was perhaps the more handsome of the pair, or so he liked to think.

"The last time you trained with me you said it was boring, not fun," Oracus mentioned.

"That's true. But I think it's wise to brush up on my sword-handling. I might need it where I'm going."

"And where are you going?" Oracus enquired hopefully.

Fortunately for Garrin, who was always dodging Oracus's questions, he was saved from answering by the arrival of their fight trainer. The trainer's name was Karvan, and he was a broad, powerful man who liked to wear only his black shorts wherever he went. His bare chest was the shade of brown leather and covered with matted black hair. The hair on his head and face was also black and wild, and his brown eyes were sheltered safely under a pair of bushy eyebrows that met at the base of his forehead. His long, muscular arms were as hairy as his chest, and his large hands were clamped around the biggest sword Oracus had ever seen.

"Find a partner!" he boomed as he opened the gate to the

training area. "Today we'll be sparring. I want you all to practise your movement. Make sure you follow my instructions and concentrate throughout. I don't want any injuries!"

Oracus and Garrin immediately paired themselves together and followed the other fighters through the open gate.

"I want you to take it easy on me today, Oracus," Garrin protested. "I don't want to be bruised for the journey."

Oracus raised his eyebrows, "You know that's not how I train. Come on, get ready."

"Has everybody got a partner?" Karvan bellowed over everyone's muttering. "Okay, get yourselves into your fighting stance and face each other."

Oracus moved swiftly into his fighting stance and held his shield in front of his body. Peering over the top of the shield, he crouched slightly and lifted his sword into position.

"To start with," Karvan continued, "I want you to practise your blocking and countering. Remember that your shield is as valuable to you as your sword. Make sure to push away your opponent's sword with it and then respond with a swift attack of your own. Begin when you're ready."

Feeling the excitement of battle engulf him, Oracus focused his eyes and began circling Garrin, challenging him to step forwards. He feigned to attack and Garrin reacted with a powerful swing of his own. Oracus stepped to the side and pushed the attack away with his shield before retaliating with a strike towards Garrin's ribs. Garrin staggered backwards but came again with another powerful blow, forcing Oracus's wooden shield to creak and protest against the assault.

For several minutes the fighting continued until Oracus's shoulders and lungs were aching and his hair was sticking to his sweaty forehead. Both Oracus and Garrin were breathing heavily and neither of them were fighting with the same vigour they had started with.

Eventually, Karvan's voice boomed over their heads, "Stop!" and Oracus dropped his sword and shield to the floor and put his hands on his hips.

Everybody in the training area halted and turned to face Karvan. Under the summer sun, they all looked as hot and flustered as Oracus, and some even sat on the dusty floor to take the weight off their feet.

"Well done, well done!" Karvan praised loudly. "Now have a break and a take a drink before we begin practising our footwork. I'll demonstrate while you recover."

Oracus and Garrin grabbed a flask of water each and stood at the edge of the training area to watch Karvan. During the whole practise, the group observed the trainer's demonstrations and repeated them with their partner. Throughout the morning, the group touched on many different techniques, and by the end of the session, Oracus was pleased with his progress. He was tired, but he felt as though his balance and positioning had improved, and he was sure Garrin could no longer keep up with him.

"I don't know how you maintain your speed," Garrin grumbled unhappily as they gulped water from their flasks and left the training area through the gate.

"That was nothing. I took it easy on you," Oracus said with a grin. "You'll have to train while you're away so we can fight again when you return."

"I'll make sure I do," Garrin assured. "I don't want you beating me by more than you already are."

They began to push their way through the many villagers who had come to inspect the merchandise being sold in the shops and stalls. Everywhere, there were people calling to one another, either shopkeepers shouting their prices or mothers disciplining their children. To Oracus's left, the sound of weapons being shaped left the open doors of the blacksmith, and to his right, he spotted his father chatting with Broid the butcher.

Oracus turned back to Garrin. "Are we still meeting tonight?"

"Does the inn at sunset suit you?" Garrin replied.

"Only if you can prove you're better at drinking than fighting."

Garrin laughed. "Then I will see you there."

At the edge of the village centre they parted company. Garrin took the path back to his home and Oracus doubled back and made a beeline for his father and Broid. No doubt his father would appreciate some help on the farm for the afternoon.

With a smile on his face, Oracus cut through the crowds of people and thought about how much he had enjoyed training with Garrin. And it wouldn't be long before sunset arrived and he could enjoy his company some more.

It was usually quite tough to find excitement in such a tiny village, but as far as days in Thessley go, Oracus considered today to have been a good day.

Three

The Storyteller

The wind swept through Oracus's hair as he walked towards the Old Mill Inn. It was cooler now, and dusk was settling over Thessley as he stepped through the shadows of the shops around him. In the daytime, the village was bustling with people, but at night it appeared abandoned. The only sign of life was the faint sound of music coming from the inn and the light than shone out of its windows.

As Oracus neared, the volume of the music increased, and the loud, drunken talk of men became audible from inside. The inn looked particularly old and haunting in the evening; the ivy growing on its face appeared black in the darkness and the windows were smeared dirt and grime.

When Oracus reached the door, the wind rattled the sign above and made him look up; it was swinging on its rusty metal arm and creaking. It was so filthy that *The Old Mill* was barely legible, and the picture of what Oracus knew to be a white windmill was lost behind the dry moss.

Without waiting, Oracus pushed open the wooden door and stepped inside. He stood in the entryway momentarily and looked around. The bar was directly opposite him and almost the length of the room, and to its left was a staircase that led to the upper floors. In front of the bar, tables and chairs occupied by men and women and their tankards were scattered about the room. And in the corner, almost hidden from view, a jolly fat man wearing a purple gown was playing a lute, the origin of the music that Oracus had heard from outside.

It appeared that Garrin had not yet arrived so Oracus ordered two tankards of ale from the barmaid and found a table near the door. At the table next to him, he realised a group of drunken men were sitting around an older man who was telling them a story. The old man's name was Elnir, and he was known as the village crackpot who told tales to earn the coin that would pay for his ale. Whenever Oracus heard mention of his name, it was usually followed by laughs and insults, but Oracus had always been interested in farfetched stories and never quite understood what was so terrible about an old man's vivid imagination. For what it was worth, he wished he could properly hear the story Elnir was telling now, but even when he leaned back in his chair, he only heard something about Riders and the icy lands in the south.

Oracus was just wondering how far to the south the icy lands might be, or if they even existed, when Garrin entered the inn. When he spotted Oracus, he made his way over and lowered himself into a vacant chair. Oracus pushed a tankard towards him and he took a quick sip. "Thank you," he said. "I've needed a drink all day."

Oracus took a gulp of his own ale and wiped the froth from his upper lip with his sleeve. "I hope you're not hurting too much from practise earlier," he teased.

"A few scratches and bruises but nothing too painful,"

Garrin answered. "I should be able to get out of bed in the morning, at least."

"What time are you leaving tomorrow?"

"Before daylight," Garrin groaned. "It'll take over a day to reach the first destination, so I need to set off as early as possible."

"And where *is* your first destination?" Oracus asked.

Garrin frowned, "I've only just got here and you're asking me about work already? You know I can't say anything."

"I just don't understand why trading is so secretive. And the less you tell me, the more I want to know!"

"It isn't the trading I can't tell you about, it's the places I go to and the people I meet. Pharia is a big place and Thessley is a very little village within it. Being secretive is what keeps it safe, you know that."

"I've wanted to know about the rest of Pharia my whole life, but nobody will say anything. I honestly don't know who knows about it and who doesn't." Oracus rolled his eyes impatiently. "Now my best friend is a tradesman and I still don't get told anything!"

"And I'm not going to," Garrin said sternly.

"You won't even tell me about the Riders and the icy lands to the south?" Oracus tried.

Garrin almost choked on his ale at Oracus's words. "Where did you hear that?" he asked, his eyes widening.

"And come to think of it, I heard something when I was younger about Pharia having a King too. Do you know anything about him?"

"Don't be so loud!" Garrin hissed, glancing over his shoulder to check that nobody was listening. "It's the King that we're keeping this village a secret from."

"So there is a King?" Oracus said with surprise. "And what about the Riders and the icy lands?"

"I don't know who told you this, Oracus, but you need to forget it."

"Forget it? How do you expect me to do that?"

"I don't know, but you shouldn't know anything about it. I could get into serious trouble if someone found out that you know."

"But-"

"Please don't beg me, Oracus. As a friend I'm asking you to let this lie." Garrin shook his head anxiously. "If I could tell you then I would. But I can't."

Oracus struggled to hide his disappointment and he looked away from Garrin. He took a gulp of his ale and wondered why it was so important for Garrin to hold his tongue, and why it was necessary to keep Thessley a secret from the King of Pharia.

There was an awkward silence between the pair for a while, in which time Garrin bought two more tankards of ale. During sips, Oracus glanced at his friend and noticed an expression of concern on his face. He looked tired too, like their earlier altercation had drained him of energy.

Suddenly, there was a bustle from the table beside them as Elnir finished telling the story to his group of rowdy listeners. There was a scraping of chair legs as the men stood and drained their tankards. Then they all stumbled from the inn, leaving Elnir by himself at his table. The old man held a half-full flagon of ale in one hand and a smoking pipe in the other, while the breast pocket of his dungarees held more silver than Oracus would know what to do with.

Forgetting about the awkwardness between them, Oracus leaned towards Garrin and lowered his voice, "Do you know anything about the stories that Elnir tells?"

Garrin appeared to become even more concerned. "I wouldn't pay attention to him," he replied. "He's a strange man who takes coin from curious people and tells them nonsense."

"You think he speaks nonsense?" Oracus pressed.

"I think he has told the stories so many times before that he believes them himself."

"But it was Elnir who I heard talking of Riders and the icy lands to the south, Garrin. Obviously not everything he speaks is a lie."

Garrin's eyes narrowed and he suddenly became very serious. "You're stepping over the line, Oracus. I asked you before not to pursue this subject but you can't help yourself." He pushed his chair back and stood up, much to Oracus's surprise. "I can't be with you when you're being like this."

"You're leaving?"

"Yes," he said bluntly. "I'll see you again when I'm home in a few weeks."

"Alright, I'm sorry!" Oracus protested. "You don't have to go."

Garrin waved his hand dismissively and moved towards the door of the inn. "Goodbye, Oracus. Enjoy your ale." And with the slam of the door behind him, he was gone.

Oracus's first thought was to follow Garrin out into the night. He felt guilty for pressing his friend for answers, and he knew he needed to apologise properly. He rose from his chair and started towards the door, but a gruff noise from behind him caught his attention. Turning around, he saw that Elnir was snoozing in his chair with his bushy white beard resting on his chest. Every time he exhaled a breath, a firm grunt swiftly followed.

In that moment, intrigue overpowered guilt, and Oracus decided not to chase Garrin. Instead, he approached Elnir and dropped noisily into the seat opposite him. "Excuse me, sir," he said loudly.

Elnir awoke with a start and his tired grey eyes took an age to adjust to Oracus's face. "What do you want?" he barked aggressively, dragging his flagon towards him as if concerned Oracus was trying to steal it. "You could kill an old man startling him like that!"

"Sorry, sir. But I was wondering if you could tell me a tale about life outside this village?" Oracus asked politely.

"You woke me to ask me that?"

"It's just that there are rumours of unusual things outside Thessley and nobody I ask seems to know anything about them."

"That's because there is nothing to know, boy. Now leave me alone!" Elnir demanded.

"I've heard you know a lot," Oracus persuaded. "And I'll pay you too, of course." He pulled a small bag of coins out his pocket and dropped it with a clunk on the table.

Elnir eyed the bag greedily but reluctantly snapped his gaze away. "I don't take money from inquisitive boys," he said forcefully.

"I'm not a boy, sir. I work for my money and I'm happy to pay to hear your stories. I assure you I'm just like any other curious listener."

Oracus pushed the money bag closer to Elnir and let him ponder for a moment. Then the old man snatched up the bag from the table and stuffed it into his already laden breast pocket. "What would you like to know?" he enquired in a much friendlier tone.

"I would like to hear about the King, sir," Oracus replied.

"Ahh, very wise choice, young man! Yes, the King!" He thought for a second, as if wondering where to start. "Do you know of the name *Jowra*?" he asked.

"No, sir."

"Then that is where I'll begin." He took a long glug from his flagon and looked far into the distance. Then his eyes snapped back onto Oracus. "A boy named Jowra lived in a village that was not unlike the one we are in now – it was hidden away in a forest where nobody knew of its existence. One day, however, King Amarad and his men discovered the village and destroyed it, killing every poor soul who lived there. All except one. Somehow, young Jowra escaped, and with his family dead, he journeyed across the land, leaving the ravaged village far behind him. After many weeks of travelling, his feet carried him into the Black Forest, an evil place that brings fear to the heart of every man, even now. Nobody knows for certain what happened to Jowra in that forest, but after entering it a weak boy, he emerged with extraordinary powers. It is said he stole the strength from the trees, but nobody knows for sure."

"What happened to him?" Oracus asked, already bubbling with intrigue and excitement.

"He travelled to King Amarad's city, of course – Melzor," Elnir replied.

"Did he kill King Amarad?" Oracus questioned impatiently.

"That was his intention, but what he hadn't expected was for King Amarad to be as powerful as himself," Elnir said.

"Had King Amarad been to the Black Forest too? Is that where his powers came from?"

"No, no, no. King Amarad had powers of a *different* kind that he had acquired years before Jowra was even born," Elnir explained. "King Amarad had bonded with a Lavorian, a creature that for centuries had only been spoken of as legend."

"A Lavorian?"

"Yes, a Lavorian. It is a creature that dedicates its life to its Rider," Elnir explained. "No two Lavorians are the same, but they resemble animals that roam freely in the forests, the deserts, the oceans and the sky. A Lavorian's metal armour is impenetrable to any weapon, and unless its Rider is killed, it is almost impossible to harm."

"Are there any Lavorians alive now?" Oracus asked hungrily.

"There are."

"Where are they?"

"There are none that live near Thessley," Elnir answered with a chuckle. "Not that I know of anyway." The old man took another mouthful of ale and some trickled through his beard. "But we have digressed somewhat… I was saying that King Amarad possessed incredible powers because of a Lavorian he had bonded with."

"Does that mean the King was stronger than Jowra?"

"I would say their strengths were very similar. But remember Jowra had the advantage of surprise. He knew he wanted to kill King Amarad, but the King knew nothing of Jowra and his powers from the Black Forest."

"So, what happened?" Oracus asked desperately.

"Well, that's where it gets a little more complicated, but certainly more interesting!" Elnir claimed, leaning forwards and enticing Oracus with a captivating smile. "Jowra moved to Melzor and found himself a job as a guard in King Amarad's palace. He gained knowledge of the King – his routines, his personality, the people he knew, the people he trusted, the powers he had, and the Lavorian he spent so much of his time with. Months had passed by when Jowra, much to his own surprise, was promoted to one of King Amarad's personal guards. Over time, he had become one of the few men the King truly trusted, and the King respected him greatly. Jowra impressed with his words and actions, he never made mistakes, and he began to influence the King's decisions. And the unsuspicious King knew nothing of Jowra's desire for revenge."

Oracus was glued to every word now. "Go on!" he said eagerly.

"On a cold, snowy night in early winter, Jowra informed King Amarad of a group of rebels that were planning an attack on Melzor. Along with himself and Jowra, the King organised some soldiers to intercept the rebels before they reached the city. Beyond the city walls, the King and Jowra separated from the soldiers, and Jowra led the King into a cave where a fight between them ensued. Jowra left King Amarad dead in that cave, and he sealed the entrance so nobody would find his body. Jowra returned to Melzor and claimed he and the King had been ambushed and he had failed to save the King's life."

"So there had never been any rebel soldiers?" Oracus asked.

"None whatsoever," Elnir replied. "And incredibly, King Amarad's death was followed by Jowra being made the new King."

"Wait, what?" Oracus stammered, his mouth gaping.

"King Amarad had no heir, and Jowra was so respected by the people of Melzor that they voted him King."

"The people didn't find out it was Jowra who had killed their King?"

"I believe the way King Amarad truly died is *still* a secret to Jowra's people, even today."

"Is Jowra still the King of Pharia now then?"

"He has been for over sixty years!" Elnir exclaimed. "And unfortunately for us, he is a King who seeks power from wherever it can be obtained. He built an army – a huge, undefeatable army – and he immediately started to take control of other cities in Pharia. He became an unstoppable force and now he rules most of the land. The only places left out of his leadership are Tallarin in the south-east, the Black Forest to the south, and the majority of the Raspian Forest here in the North."

"Why doesn't anyone try to resist him?" Oracus asked.

"He isn't just handed villages and cities and told to enjoy them!" Elnir joked. "But it's difficult to resist a man as powerful as he is. Jowra has everything he needs to rule the land because his power has no limits. When a mere Human kills a Rider, as Jowra had killed King Amarad, he will inherit the dead Rider's powers and also bond with the Rider's Lavorian. The moment King Amarad died, Jowra acquired *his* incredible powers, in addition to those he already had. And a Lavorian too!"

"But what's the difference between a Human and a Rider?" Oracus asked.

"A Human is what you and I are – just normal folk. But there are also many other creatures in Pharia that are neither Human nor Rider. A Rider is the name given to those, whether Human or otherwise, who have forged a bond with a Lavorian," Elnir explained. "And a Lavorian is ridden by its Rider in battle."

"There are other creatures in Pharia too?" Oracus questioned, feeling more and more shocked.

"Of course! But not in this forest. They're in other areas of Pharia you'll likely never see."

"What types of creatures are they? And can you tell me how a bond is made with a Lavorian too?"

Elnir laughed and then hiccuped. "You paid me to talk of the King, not Lavorians and other creatures. But you should know that boys like you from small, hidden villages in large forests don't ever bond with Lavorians. It's Jowra who decides who becomes a Rider."

Oracus couldn't help but feel slightly downhearted about that. The thought of becoming a Rider was quite an exciting one. Nevertheless, he was determined to get his money's worth from Elnir, so he persevered with his questions. "Is Thessley safe from King Jowra?" he asked, remembering what Garrin had said about keeping the village a secret.

Elnir raised his eyebrows at the question, "We're well hidden and we've been safe here for a very long time. There's no reason why that should change."

"But what if he did find us here?" Oracus pressed.

"Then, quite frankly, we wouldn't stand a chance. Huge cities have surrendered to him before now."

Something about the way Elnir spoke made Oracus shiver, and he felt goosepimples rise on his arms. "There's one thing about King Jowra I don't understand though," he said. "Why does he destroy lives by invading villages and cities when his family were killed during an invasion by King Amarad? Does he not realise he's punishing them in the same way *he* was punished?"

"That is a very good question," Elnir said, "and unfortunately I don't have an answer for it. Maybe it's psychosis or insanity that drives him to it. Or maybe it's that he wants everyone else to feel a similar pain to what he felt when his family were slaughtered."

"The longer we talk about it, the worse it sounds," Oracus stated.

"You're right. I think now is actually a good place to stop," Elnir said, rubbing his eyes and standing up. "I'm drunk, I'm tired, and I need to sleep."

"But I paid you to tell me," Oracus argued.

"And I've told you more than I intended to," the old man retorted. "You got a great deal more than your little bag of coins was worth."

"Just another few questions?" Oracus pleaded hopefully.

"I bid you goodnight!" Elnir replied with finality. He wobbled slightly as he stepped away from the table, but then limped with purpose to the door and hobbled out into the night without giving Oracus another glance.

Following Elnir's abrupt departure, Oracus stayed seated for a while. He stared down into the dregs of his ale and retold the old man's story to himself several times until even the lute-player had left the inn. Eventually, the tinkle of glasses being cleaned behind the bar snapped him from his thoughts, and after realising that he was the only punter still there, he lifted himself out of his chair and exited the inn himself. Thoughts were still whirring, but he longed for his bed.

FOUR

An Unexpected Appearance

Oracus struggled to sleep that night, and the few times he did drift he was plagued by unpleasant dreams. Maybe it had been wise of Garrin not to answer his questions about Pharia, because now Oracus wished he hadn't listened to Elnir. Talking to the old man hadn't satisfied his curiosity as he'd hoped, it had just made him feel anxious instead.

The stories that Elnir told seemed farfetched, but somehow believable, and Oracus could find no reason to disbelieve him, even with Elnir being known as the crackpot village storyteller. But surely Oracus would have found out before now if there were magical powers and creatures of fantasy around Pharia. Or maybe he wouldn't.

Oracus untangled himself from the sheets of his bed. It was long before the sun was due to rise but he needed to walk while he thought. He dressed and left the house quietly, not wanting to wake his father, and proceeded down the street towards the forest. He had often been into the forest to walk and hunt, even at night. But tonight it felt different somehow, like an uneasiness lingered within it. And the moment Oracus stepped between the trees, the hairs on his neck stood and he felt the eyes of the creatures in the branches above glaring at him with mistrust.

For a second, Elnir's stories left Oracus's mind and he considered returning home; never had he felt such uncertainty. There was a cold gust of wind that rustled the leaves overhead and the crowing of a bird that was strangely unfamiliar to him. But with a defiant shake of his head, he pressed on into the forest until the path fell into thick undergrowth and dense shrubbery.

Soon enough, the unusual feel of the forest was forgotten and Oracus's thoughts of Pharia began to battle with themselves again. Had Elnir been truthful in his tales, or did he just earn money from the stupid, the curious and the gullible as Garrin had warned? Maybe his stories were an exaggerated truth where the powers and the fairy-tale creatures were made up, but the maniacal King Jowra was real. Oracus's uneasiness became fright as he imagined a tyrannous man with a sword slaying everyone in his path. He wanted to believe that Thessley was safe, but ultimately, whether magic existed or not, it was utterly defenceless against a powerful King who was intent on destroying it. And what would become of his father and friends if that were to happen? There was nobody to protect them, and nobody to save them should the worst happen.

Horrific visions suddenly burst into Oracus's thoughts and he found himself struggling to breathe. He saw his father fall dead at the feet of merciless soldiers and he watched Garrin drop to his knees and beg for his life to be spared. He heard the screams of terrified women and children, and saw fires and chaos devastate Thessley until it was nothing more than rubble and ash underfoot. Oracus screamed into the night as pain immersed his entire body and he dropped helplessly to the floor. A world of despairing darkness flashed past his eyes, and unbearable agony caused him to convulse on the ground. Then, as calm washed over his fragile frame, he opened his eyes and wondered if death had released him.

He was standing now, and the forest was no longer dark. In fact, it was lighter than Oracus had ever known. He squinted blindly for a moment before his eyes adjusted to a woman standing in front of him. The shock of her sudden appearance made him step backwards, but then he gaped at her angelic beauty. The woman was tall and slender with flowing blonde hair and blue eyes that glistened within her beautiful but ageing face. Her white robe, which was short enough to reveal bare feet beneath it, matched the brightness of the light around her. With a caring smile, she moved delicately towards Oracus and placed a warm hand on his cheek. Her soft fingertips caressed his skin and she held his gaze for a moment. Then a teardrop fell from her eye and her smile was gone.

A deafening clap of thunder suddenly ripped Oracus from his dream. The forest was dark once again and the glow of the woman was nowhere to be seen. Lightning flashed overhead, and rain fell in sheets onto a sodden forest floor. Oracus was lying alone in a puddle on the edge of a clearing, with a dull pain throbbing in his muscles and the cold rain biting at his skin. He tried to remember how he had got there and wondered how long he had been unconscious for. And he briefly considered who the woman had been.

Another louder clap of thunder made him look up at the

sky – it was scarred by white bolts of lightning and purple flashes. And there, between the flashes, a single orange star glided across the black canvas. From where he lay, Oracus marvelled at the star and felt curiosity take over him. More flashes of lightning came and then the star appeared to change direction. Oracus twisted his body to observe the star's movements, but then he yelled out as it became larger and brighter, and whistled towards the clearing at incredible speed.

With a crash that shook the forest floor and sent earth flying in every direction, the star collided with the ground. Oracus threw up his hands to protect his head, and yelled until the ground ceased to quake. When he felt that it was safe to look, he peered through his fingers and stumbled to his feet.

What had landed before him made him stare in disbelief. It was an object of such a peculiar oval shape that he wondered if it could even be a star. It was more like a rock that had been carved and polished, and then dropped from the sky. But running through the rock were pulsating veins of amber that radiated warmth like the log fire in Oracus's house.

Oracus now had more concerns than when he had started his walk in the forest. Not only was he worried about Elnir's stories of the King, he was scared for his own immediate safety too. All these strange occurrences couldn't just be mere coincidence – the agony he had endured when imagining Thessley's destruction, the woman he had dreamed about, the rock that had fallen from the sky and was now glowing in front of him. Even the air of the forest had felt different when he first entered it.

Oracus wished he was back at home and wrapped up in a blanket on his comfortable bed. The rain continued to fall, and the flashes of lightning repeatedly lit up the sky. He was cold, wet and scared, with anxiety brewing in his bones. He needed to leave the forest and get far away from the clearing.

But when he turned to escape, a loud bang echoed in the darkness and a blinding silver light escaped from a crack in the centre of the rock. Oracus shielded his eyes until the brightness had dimmed, and then he noticed that the rock had broken in half. Lying between the pieces was a creature unlike anything he had ever seen before; it was a Lion cub as small and fragile as a newborn, but with silver metal fur instead of golden. Despite the torrential rain, it lifted its tiny head and searched for Oracus with its yellow eyes. Suddenly, the storm above ceased and silence swept over the clearing. In that moment, Oracus realised he was no longer scared or anxious, but fascinated.

Without taking his eyes off it, he slowly approached the cub until he was just an arm's length away. "It's okay," he whispered comfortingly. "I won't hurt you." He knelt and reached out a steady hand until his fingertips touched its head. "I'll look after you now," he reassured.

For a short time, the Lion cub did nothing. But then it pressed its head into the palm of Oracus's hand and purred quietly. In that instant, the silence of the forest ended and the rain began to fall again.

FIVE

Saviour From The Sky

Choosing a name was difficult, Oracus thought. He must have considered and ultimately rejected a thousand names for the Lion-like creature in the last few hours, and he still couldn't make up his mind.

It was mid-afternoon, and he was in a run-down barn at the far side of his father's farmland, lying on a spilled bale of hay with the cub curled up beside him. He had been in the barn since daybreak, with his sodden clothes slowly drying after he had carried the Lion through the forest in the storm. With Thessley being so small, the barn was the only place Oracus knew that would keep the cub out of sight from the locals – nobody but Oracus and his father had been there in several years.

Other than a few murmurs, the Lion hadn't stirred from its sleep, but Oracus had struggled to keep his eyes off it. With metal fur protecting its whole body and silver teeth and claws like tiny knives, it was a creature he couldn't help but admire. Watching its chest rise and fall with every sleepy breath, he wondered for hours what it was, and where it might have come from. He had never heard of rocks falling from the sky before, and he had never known of curious beasts being born from rocks either. But what concerned Oracus most of all was that the rock and creature seemed to have fallen *for* him, either by luck or mistake. And he had no idea what he was supposed to do about it.

But it wasn't just the appearance of the Lion that worried Oracus, he was also unsure how the villagers would react should they discover it. He doubted they would want to do anything other than kill it and discard of it. Anything out of the ordinary was frowned upon in Thessley, much like knowledge of the rest of Pharia, or Elnir's foolish stories. But Oracus felt a strange connection with the creature, and he had no intention of giving it up, no matter how forceful the villagers might be.

Oracus fidgeted anxiously and the cub slowly roused from its repose. It looked up at him with sleepy yellow eyes, then rose to its feet and stretched. After raising its head and sniffing the air, it padded carefully across the barn with its nose pressed against the ground. Within seconds, its alert body had stiffened and it began to prowl towards the corner of the barn with unblinking concentration. Oracus watched in awe as the cub leaped and dived at the floor with astonishing speed, and then trotted triumphantly towards him with a limp mouse in its jaws.

Oracus gasped as a thought suddenly struck him. The Lion had reminded him of a line written in *The Beasts of Legend*:

Undetectable and silent, the Bandor only ever reveals itself when its teeth are clamped securely around its victim's throat.

"Bandor!" Oracus shouted happily. "Your name is Bandor!"

The Lion purred, and then started to tear into the helpless mouse's flesh.

It hadn't occurred to Oracus that Bandor might require food. And now he doubted that the infestation of rodents would keep him sufficiently nourished for more than a couple of days. Oracus would have to travel into the Raspian Forest and hunt. And with an extra mouth to feed than just himself and his father, he would need more than just a few rabbits, he would probably need a deer.

"I'm going to get you some more food," Oracus said, getting up. Bandor looked at him briefly, with blood dripping down his silver chin. "You're not to leave this barn, okay?"

Unsurprisingly, there was no reply, but Oracus somehow knew that the Lion had understood him. He paused for a moment and grimaced as the last of the meat was removed from the mouse's tiny bones, then turned on his heels and left.

Oracus ate and bathed at home before grabbing his bow and arrows for the hunting trip in the forest. The forest seemed more welcoming in the daylight, with birdsong floating through the branches and the scent of flowers rich in the air. But the strange occurrences from the night before still left Oracus feeling wary.

As the undergrowth thickened and the bright sunlight was hindered by a denser canopy above, Oracus spotted hoof marks in the dirt and signs that deer had been feeding on the bushes around him. All concerns of the forest left him as he focused on the spoor. It appeared that the herd had been spooked recently and fled east, leaving distinctive tracks in their wake. Oracus quickly pursued the deer and hoped they hadn't travelled too far; dragging a whole deer carcass for miles through the forest would take hours or days, time that he would rather spend back in Thessley with Bandor.

After an hour of pushing through the trees and bushes as fast as he could, Oracus sensed that he was nearing his prey. He slowed to a halt, listened cautiously, and then crept for a while longer until he spotted two bucks and four doe drinking from a stream in a clearing. Still undetected and hidden behind the trees, Oracus carefully slid an arrow from his quiver and nocked it to his bowstring. He chose the smallest of the females as his target and focused his aim. But as he drew the arrow back towards his cheek, the herd sensed a threat and scattered. In a moment of panic, Oracus released the arrow and watched it sail harmlessly past the deer and into the forest beyond. The deer escaped into the trees, and Oracus was left to toss his bow aside in frustration.

He slumped against the trunk of a tree and sighed. He had been so close. Now he would have to pursue the deer further into the forest or locate another herd nearer to Thessley. For a while longer, he sat and thought, then he approached the stream to take a drink. The clearing through which the stream passed was filled with the sound of trickling water. Trees in the clearing were sparse, but colourful flowers sprouted near the water's edge and mushrooms were grouped in the damp shadows of dead stumps. Where the trees were missing, sunlight shone down and bounced off the surface of the water, filling the air with warmth.

As Oracus stood after quenching his thirst, he took a deep breath and tasted smoke on the breeze. He looked around himself, puzzled. Then the distant blast of an unfamiliar horn made his heart stop in his chest.

Apprehension flooded his body, and he found himself dashing out of the clearing and towards the origin of the noise. For half a mile, he ran, and the scent of the smoke became stronger with every step he took until he found himself on the brim of a huge hollow that looked down at dozens of grand white tents with hundred of soldiers stomping between them.

The soldiers wore crimson battle robes and armour, with swords on their waists and metal shields strapped to their backs. Each one looked fierce and unpleasant, unlike anyone Oracus had seen before in Thessley, and at the centre of them all, a colossal campfire billowed black smoke high into the sky.

Oracus watched the camp for as long as he dared. The soldiers were loud and aggressive, often breaking into fights amongst themselves. And if they weren't beating each other with fists, they were cutting chunks of meat off a wild boar that had been spitroasted over the fire, or downing flagons of ale. When Oracus had seen enough, he left the hollow behind him and ran as fast as he could back to Thessley, hoping the people of the village would believe him when he told them soldiers were stationed in the forest.

After what seemed like hours, Oracus stumbled onto the path that led to his house and gulped deep breaths of air.

The orange sun was lowering behind the thatched houses as he bounded over the gate and crashed through his front door. He shouted for his father, but it looked like the house had been empty for several hours, so he knocked on the doors of his neighbours, but all those houses appeared vacant too.

Oracus's worry soon became panic. Desperate to find someone, he rushed to the village centre and found all the shops and stalls dark and deserted; even the Old Mill was void of light and music. He spun around and squinted into the windows of the shops, hoping that someone would jump out and yell "Surprise!" at the top of their voice. But it was clear this was no elaborate joke. Thessley had been abandoned, and Oracus was all by himself.

Sheer desperation had now set in, and Oracus wondered what had driven the villagers away. Had they already been warned of the soldiers in the forest? Had they seen the smoke rising into the sky from their camp maybe? Or was it because–

"Oh no," Oracus uttered to himself. "Bandor!"

Oracus was swiftly on the move again, bundling through his father's farmhouse and into the field behind, pleading silently that the Lion was still in the derelict barn. He raced across the grass, which was now in the shadow of dusk, and heard a voice bellow at him from the farmhouse he had just ran through.

Oracus stopped in his tracks and turned, hoping it was a villager who had shouted him. Instead, he found himself staring at four muscular soldiers in red armour, all wearing helmets that covered their heads and faces.

Together, the soldiers advanced, and one of them

removed his helmet. He bellowed again, this time with words that Oracus could understand. "What is your business here, boy?"

All four soldiers drew their swords as they neared, and Oracus gasped as he saw how grotesque the leader was. A broad, bald man with a face so badly scarred it barely resembled a face. He had only one ear and his nose had been partially cut off, and all but three of his teeth were missing from a slanted mouth.

"What is your business here, boy?" the monstrous man repeated impatiently.

Oracus's hands began to shake and his heart thundered in his chest. He was terrified, but he tried his best not to show it. "This is my village," he shouted. "I live here."

The man looked around and shrugged. "Do you live here alone? I see nobody else."

"No, a lot of people live here. And you'll be sorry when they return!"

The man turned to his accomplices and laughed loudly. "We'll kill anybody who opposes us," he said. "And a handful of peasants wielding sticks won't scare us."

Oracus could see the men were far from concerned by his threat. And maybe it wasn't wise of him to be so hostile when he was standing alone against them. "Then take whatever you want and leave," he offered.

The man gave a lopsided smile. "Give us the Lavorian and we'll be on our way."

The proposal was such an unexpected one it took Oracus's breath away. A Lavorian? The creature that Elnir had mentioned during his story the night before? Hadn't he said the King had total control over the Lavorians and who became their Riders? Surely the soldier was mistaken.

And then it was like someone flicked a switch in Oracus's head. How had he not realised it before? Bandor was a Lavorian! He was exactly as Elnir had described. And the man in the field was demanding to be given Bandor so he could take him back to the King.

Oracus's mind was suddenly spinning so quickly that he struggled to comprehend everything he had learned during the last day. But the one thing he was sure about was that he wasn't willing to hand Bandor over, especially to men who hadn't been invited into his village. Feeling a surge of hatred and reckless courage, he no longer cared for stalling the soldiers – he wanted them dead.

Without consideration, he pulled the bow from his back, nocked an arrow to the string and fired it at the grotesque soldier's face. The arrow was shot perfectly, but with the speed and precision of nothing Oracus had seen before, the man unsheathed his sword and swatted it away like an annoying fly.

"Wrong move, boy," the man said fiercely.

Oracus's bow-arm slumped to his side as the four men all started to advance. He wanted to load another arrow, but he was too scared to move. Dread had turned his limbs heavy, and he was sure his life was about to end. The darkness closed in on him, and trepidation gnawed at his bones.

"Please, I don't want to die!" he begged.

But as the words left his mouth, a ferocious shriek erupted from the sky above and brought the four soldiers to a halt. They looked blindly into the night and Oracus's spirits rose. Then, without warning, two of the four were wrenched out of sight by a huge creature Oracus couldn't make out in the darkness. Terrified screams echoed all around the field until silence fell. Then a gust of wind ruffled Oracus's hair as the unseen beast shot past him with astonishing speed and carried the third soldier into the night, leaving the deformed man all alone.

"Show yourself!" the man demanded as he swung his sword hopelessly through the air.

Another screech pierced the night and a huge creature descended from the sky. Oracus fell backwards in fear, while the soldier took several steps back at the sight of his enemy.

When the beast's claws touched the ground, Oracus could see it was a bird of some kind, but it stood taller than him and had wings as wide as three barns. The bird's beak looked as sharp as any weapon, and it carried the same armour as Bandor, yet the bird's armour was not of fur, but feathers. Looking closely, Oracus noticed the bird resembled the Eagles he had sometimes seen soaring over the canopy of the Raspian Forest whilst hunting. But this Eagle was much larger, and it had a bridle circling its head, with reins being held by a Rider on its saddled back.

"You should not be here," the Rider shouted forcefully at the soldier. He dismounted the Eagle and pulled his silver sword free of its sheath. Oracus could not see his face, but his hair was blonde and wavy. "Leave now or I will kill you."

The soldier gathered himself and puffed out his chest. "There are hundreds of soldiers ready to take over this village. Do you plan to kill them all?"

"I gave you a chance," the Rider said coolly. Then he

swiftly moved towards the soldier, knocked aside his raised weapon, and thrust a fatal stab into his heart. He held his sword in place for long enough to see the life drain from his victim's eyes, and then slowly withdrew it, leaving the once powerful man to slump lifelessly onto the ground.

For a short time, the Rider kept his back to Oracus, as if deliberately keeping his identity a secret.

"Who are you?" Oracus stammered.

Eventually, the Rider turned around and revealed a familiar face that Oracus hadn't expected.

"Garrin?"

His best friend was stood before him with blood on his hands and a glumness in his eyes. He looked exhausted and apprehensive.

Oracus remained on the ground, worried his legs wouldn't support him if he stood. "Garrin, what's going on?"

"I can't tell you here, Oracus. We need to leave."

"You just killed that man!" Oracus stated, pointing at the dead body on the grass by Garrin's feet.

"Seriously, we need to go," Garrin urged.

With shock preventing him adhering to his friend's order, Oracus switched his attention to the Eagle. "Is that a Lavorian?"

"Oracus, listen to me. In a few minutes this field will be full of soldiers wanting to kill us. If we don't go now, we might not leave with our lives."

Garrin's plead brought Oracus to his senses and he pushed himself unsteadily to his feet. "What shall we do then?" he asked.

Garrin sheathed his sword and marched towards the

Eagle. "Ride together," he said.

Oracus began to follow, but then remembered Bandor was still in the barn. He couldn't just leave him there for the soldiers to find. "Garrin, wait for me!" he shouted.

Before Garrin could respond, Oracus had set off at a sprint towards the barn. When he reached the door, he kicked it open and rushed inside, and found Bandor waiting patiently for his return.

"We're leaving," Oracus said simply. He scooped Bandor into his arms and crashed back out the door again.

As the night air hit Oracus's face, he heard the bellow of a nearby horn and spotted a hundred fiery torches floating onto the field. Panic began to set in, and he ran as fast as he could back to where Garrin and the Eagle were waiting.

When Oracus reached them, Garrin helped him onto the Eagle's back and then pulled himself into the saddle, just as the soldiers were beginning to close in.

"Brace yourself," Garrin warned, and the Eagle spread its gigantic wings and took off.

Cold wind washed over Oracus's skin as the Eagle rose. Beneath them, outraged shouts left the mouths of the soldiers, and arrows were loosed from their bows. Many of the arrows clanged against the Eagle's metal underbelly, but some whistled past Oracus's ears and into the darkness above.

Finally, as Thessley and the soldiers were left behind, Oracus breathed a huge sigh of relief. It had been touch and go for a moment, but he had somehow escaped with his life. Just.

SIX

From Safety To Sorrow

Oracus, Garrin and the two creatures descended sooner than Oracus had expected. Initially, the dense Raspian Forest was all they could make out beneath them in the darkness. But before long, the forest was replaced by flat, empty grassland, and the horizon surrendered dozens of hazy amber lights.

As they approached the lights, Oracus's anxiety peaked. What had at first been a few innocuous lights in the distance turned out to be a place far greater than Thessley. It was a magnificent city like those he had read in his storybooks. From such a height, he could see almost all the city beyond its colossal outer-wall. There were hundreds of buildings, mostly made of yellow stone, but some towards the rear of the city that were wooden and thatched like those in Thessley. Between the buildings, the bustle of city-folk was impossible to miss, even in the darkness. There were markets and stalls in every spare space, and the occasional lonely tree growing out of the sandy ground.

The Eagle descended with Oracus, Garrin and Bandor towards an opening in the wall that was protected by a moat, drawbridge and portcullis. When its claws met the ground, Oracus looked up at the archers who manned the top of the wall, and then he peered down into the ominous black water that separated him from the city. He slid from the Eagle's back and placed Bandor on the grassy floor, then started to wretch.

He felt Garrin's gentle hand on his back. "Are you alright?" he asked.

"I'm fine," Oracus said. "It's all come as a bit of a shock, that's all."

"Take a deep breath and try to relax. We'll stay here until you're ready."

Behind Oracus, the sound of flapping metal wings began, and the Eagle took flight and glided over the wall, leaving Oracus, Garrin and Bandor alone. In the next moment, the chains of the drawbridge started to crank along with the rise of the portcullis.

"I think I'm ready," Oracus said, wiping his mouth with his sleeve.

"Come on then," Garrin urged. "Follow me."

Oracus cradled Bandor again, and when the drawbridge clunked to the ground, he cautiously followed Garrin across. The archers were now aiming their arrows down at the bridge, and Oracus felt another pang of sickness. Beyond the opening portcullis, an elderly man in a green robe waited.

"I found him at last," Garrin said to the man as they approached him.

"I was starting to think that you wouldn't return," the man responded.

"It was a close one. The soldiers had reached the village."

Garrin nodded his head at Oracus. "And this brave fool was defending it all by himself."

The man in green turned to Oracus, then his eyes dropped to Bandor. "Goodness gracious!" he exclaimed. "Another Lavorian! You didn't say your friend was a Rider too, Garrin."

"I didn't actually know," Garrin replied. "It seems I'm not the only one from Thessley who's good at keeping secrets."

The man's eyes were glistening with emotion as he held out a shaking hand to Oracus. "It's very nice to meet you, young man. You are very welcome here in Afarra."

Oracus took the man's hand but couldn't find the words to respond. The man had just called him a Rider, and he could feel the shock taking over his body again.

"Do you mind if we pass through?" Garrin asked the man. "This is all very new to him and I want to get him to safety as quickly as possible."

"Of course, of course!" The man moved aside to let them by. "It's such a pleasure to have you here. Enjoy your stay."

Beyond the portcullis, Afarra was full of life. The market stalls Oracus had seen from the sky were even more abundant than he had realised. And the noise that the many people made was cacophonous.

"Be careful here, Oracus," Garrin advised. "The moment they spot your Lavorian they'll begin to form a crowd. Follow me and I'll guide you away from the mayhem."

"I want to see my father," Oracus shouted over the loud voices around him.

"That's where I'm taking you," Garrin shouted back.

Indeed, Garrin was right. For a short time, Oracus weaved between people without receiving attention. But then Bandor was spotted by a young boy and suddenly half of the city seemed to descend upon them. Within seconds, hands were groping for both Oracus and Bandor, and men and women of all ages were yelling gratefully to them and cheering. Garrin tried his utmost to forge a path through the crowd, but then he seemed to be recognised too and was swept up by the horde.

It seemed like hours had passed before Oracus eventually escaped into a narrow alleyway with Garrin and Bandor. Still the crowd converged, but with less force in a more confined space.

When the noise had lessened and Oracus could finally hear himself think, they reached a small house with crumbling walls and a dull grey door. Garrin advanced towards the house and pulled Oracus inside. He then closed the door behind them, blocking out the voices of the remaining people who had followed them along the alleyway.

"Not what you were expecting, I suppose?" Garrin said with a tired smile.

"Why were they all acting like that?" Oracus asked, breathing heavily.

"It's not often a new Rider and Lavorian come to the city. In fact, its very rare indeed." Garrin yawned and then looked at the door they'd just come through. "We're like royalty to the people out there."

Oracus looked aimlessly around the room they were in while he took in Garrin's words. There was a thick layer of dust on the stone floor and not much else. There was a spiral staircase leading to the floor above that was adjacent to the back door, and an overbearing musty smell that was unpleasant in the nose.

"How did this happen?" Garrin questioned, glancing between Oracus and Bandor. "Where did you find him?"

"I was in the forest when he fell out of the sky in a rock and almost crushed me," Oracus replied. "Is it because of us that the soldiers found Thessley?"

Garrin grimaced and nodded. "The King tracks the falling rocks and sends his soldiers to retrieve them. When they saw the Lavorian was missing, they searched the area of surrounding forest and encountered the village."

"I'm sorry. I didn't mean for any of this to happen," Oracus said glumly.

"We got everyone out of Thessley alive, that's what matters," Garrin assured. "Afarra's soldiers completed the evacuation just as we'd planned."

"I guess being a tradesman was a cover for whatever you're doing here?" Oracus supposed.

Garrin looked away from Oracus and rubbed his hands together anxiously. "Your father is upstairs. You should go and see him. There are some important issues elsewhere I need to go and address."

Suddenly, Garrin had left through the back door and Oracus was alone in the dusty room with Bandor. As he prepared to ascend the stairs to see his father, he couldn't help but think how rocky his and Garrin's friendship had become. They had shared everything with each other as children, but since Garrin had started leaving Thessley for *business,* Oracus felt like everything had become so secretive. Had they been younger, Garrin would never have lied to him about becoming a Rider – they would undoubtedly have enjoyed that adventure together.

At the top of the spiral staircase was a small landing and an entry to a bedroom that was as dusty as the room below it. Stepping inside, there was only a bed to look at, and Oracus's father was lying asleep upon it.

Oracus placed Bandor on the floor and approached the bed. His footsteps clunked on the wooden floorboards and his father stirred from the noise. Through sleepy eyes, he gazed at Oracus and a weak smile crossed his lips.

"Oracus!" he gasped. "Thank goodness."

Oracus knelt beside his father and kissed him on his bearded cheek. "Are you alright?" he asked. "You look pale."

"I'm just a bit sore. Nothing to worry about."

"Sore? Why, what happened? And why are you in here all alone?"

Oracus's father waved a hand. "I sent them away for fussing around me." He tried to sit up, but groaned in pain and lay back down.

"You're not telling me something," Oracus said sternly. "You're hurt."

"It's just a small wound."

"Show me," Oracus insisted.

"No!" his father protested. "I'm fine."

"Let me see!" Oracus lifted his father's shirt and revealed a wound on his stomach he'd tried to bandage himself. From behind the dressing, black lines of infection crawled across his torso from his shoulders to his hips. "This is serious, father!" Oracus exclaimed. "Why are you hiding this?"

"There's nothing anyone can do to heal it, son. The poison was already in my blood when they found me."

"Poison? Who did this to you?"

"The soldiers in the forest," his father answered.

"What were you thinking?" Oracus shouted. "You never go into the forest!"

"The village was being evacuated and nobody had seen you! Where was I supposed to go?"

"Not in there!" Oracus cried. He could feel a lump growing in his throat and tears began to well in his eyes.

"But I couldn't leave you behind, you're my son! I wouldn't have been able to forgive myself if you'd died."

Tears trickled down his father's cheeks and Oracus began to sob. His chest tightened and he found himself struggling to breathe. "I need to find someone who can help you," he stuttered.

"It's too late for that now. I can already feel the poison entering my heart. There's nothing anyone can do for me." His father's eyes closed and he struggled to open them again. "I've been fighting it for hours, waiting to see if you're okay. And now I know you're safe..."

"No! This can't be happening!" Oracus groaned. "I can't lose you, I need you here."

"You don't need me, son. You're stronger than you realise." He lifted a shaking hand and pointed at Bandor. "You're a Rider now. Your Lavorian will keep you safe."

Oracus looked into his father's eyes – the eyes that reflected the green of his own – and saw knowledge within them. "You know what he is?"

"There's a lot I know that I never told you, son. I was a fool to keep it all a secret from you." His father's voice was hoarse now, and he gasped with every word. "I don't have the time to tell you now. But I'm sure you will find the answers for yourself when I'm gone."

"You aren't going anywhere! Don't say that!" Oracus pleaded.

His father used the last of his strength to touch Oracus's cheek with his fingers. "I couldn't have wished for a better son. I love you so much."

And with one final shallow breath, his hand fell to the bed and his dazzling green eyes closed forever.

SEVEN

A King's Daughter

Catania was locked in a dark, damp dungeon with the unbearable cold biting her bare flesh. The only source of light was from a tiny, barred window where a slither of white moonlight was cast onto the squalid floor. She was forced to stand in her chains, with shackles around her wrists linked to the ceiling and manacles weighing down her feet, while the other prisoners were boxed in cages along the walls that would have been too small even for dogs.

Catania had been in the dungeon for three whole days. In that time, she hadn't once been fed, or indeed seen anyone other than the caged captives around her. She had watched the steel door for hours at a time, and occasionally turned her attention to the rats that prowled from shadow to shadow. Even whilst standing she was fighting sleep, but she didn't dare to close her eyes and leave herself vulnerable. And neither did she think she would cope if her dreams were a repeat of Alticon's death.

When the moon appeared to be at its brightest, darkness briefly washed over the moonlit floor and Catania lifted her head expectantly. Two bangs of a lock followed by a slow creak echoed loudly within the dungeon, and the scent of fresh air floated into the room. Catania squinted at two men who were stood together in the doorway, one much taller and slimmer than the short, pot-bellied other, and her heart began to pound in her chest.

Immediately, pleads for freedom from the caged prisoners commenced, but Catania knew the two men were seeking her. She stared fearfully while they lingered at a distance, and then gasped as the taller man glided towards her.

"You look weak, Catania," his voice rasped evilly when he reached her. Even in the darkness, his crimson eyes glowed with malice. "Who would have thought a daughter of mine could look so pathetic?"

Catania withdrew from him as far as her shackles would allow. She didn't want to look at his pale face, nor smell the dampness in his greasy black hair.

The man's lipless mouth contorted into a sinister smile. "It's been a long time, my child. I was beginning to wonder if I would ever see you again." He paused and stroked her cheek with his dexterous fingers. "If memory serves me correctly, you left all those years ago with something that belonged to me." His scarlet eyes looked deep into Catania's soul. "The Lavorian, Catania! You stole the Lavorian!"

"You tortured him!" Catania snapped, feeling anger building inside her.

"Do not shout at me!" the man bellowed. He struck her twice across the face with his hand. "I am your King! Learn to respect me!"

Catania cried out in pain and dropped her eyes to the floor, her anger subsiding. The man's rage eased too, and he ran his fingers gently over the red marks on her face. Suddenly Catania was back to feeling frightened, and she shirked away from his touch.

"A King should expect his people to follow him and fight for him," the man said in a calm whisper that Catania could not fail to understand. "The majority of them do. But some feel it is necessary to oppose me. Such rebels cause me a problem, Catania, because they make my land imperfect. And as you know only too well, I despise imperfection." He ran a frustrated hand through his waxy hair. "So, I'll give you a very reasonable choice. Either command your people to surrender to their King, as they should, or I will march my soldiers into your city and kill every man, woman and child who lives there."

"Threaten me all you like," Catania said, discovering the last of her courage. "We both know you don't have the strength to invade my city, or you would have done so already. And don't think you can torture me into submission either, I will never make my people bow to you."

"Oh, your predictability is astonishing," the man replied with a bored shake of his head. "You didn't think I'd actually threaten you without sufficient leverage, did you?" His thin mouth curled into a smile again. "I *could* march my soldiers into your city and force you to surrender, but that would be a waste of precious men. So how about this…?" He began to pace backwards and forwards as he spoke. "Why don't you give me control of your people in return for the freedom of your precious wolf?"

Catania gulped. "But Alticon is dead. Your men killed him in the forest when they captured me."

"No, no, no! I wouldn't have let them kill him," the man assured. "Not when I could use him against you like this."

As if on cue, a howl of pain came from outside the dungeon door. Catania tugged at the shackles and cried out in despair.

"So, what do you say now?" the man urged, his red eyes bulging sadistically. "I could cause him a lot of discomfort, or you could just agree to cooperate."

Catania stopped struggling against her bonds and sagged in defeat. There was nothing she could do to deny the King now. "I'll do whatever you want," she conceded. "Just don't hurt him anymore. Please."

The man clapped his hands together triumphantly. "Wonderful!" He stepped away from Catania and moved towards where the short, fat man was still standing in the doorway. "Unbind her, Riskin," he ordered. "We're taking my daughter back to the palace."

Eight

A Lavorian's Voice

More than four-hundred people attended the funeral of Oracus's father. In a vast cemetery full of old gravestones, flowers and oak trees, most of the villagers from Thessley were present, and even some citizens of Afarra had come to pay their respects.

The midday sun shone down on the crowd as they gathered around the grave, and everyone listened to the stories that were told by those who Oracus's father had known best. For most of the ceremony, Oracus had tried his hardest to stem the tears, but during his speech he hadn't been able to hold back the sobs of despair.

The man who had taught him everything was dead. Gone forever. It had been his father who had showed him how to use a bow and arrow, let him assist with caring for the livestock on the farm, and helped him to get a job at the blacksmith's workshop in Thessley's village centre. Never again would he listen to his father's voice or hear his advice.

When the ceremony reached its climax, the coffin was lowered into the grave and soil was shovelled over it.

Oracus tried to offer some final grateful words, but his throat tightened, and the words never came. He sobbed harder than he had ever sobbed in his life, and he felt Garrin's arm wrap around his shoulder.

"Don't blame yourself for what happened," he was told. "There's nothing anyone could have done to stop this."

I could have not gone hunting in the forest in the first place, Oracus thought. *Or I could have ran home when the Lavorian fell from the sky.*

Garrin's grip stiffened and Oracus rested his head on his friend's shoulder. "Life was simple," he said, trying to hold his voice steady. "But now all this has happened and I don't know what to do."

"I'm sorry, Oracus, but I don't think life will ever be simple now you're a Rider."

"But I don't know if I want that, Garrin. I had a good life back in Thessley. Since Bandor showed up I've lost my father and lost Thessley too. And I nearly got killed myself. What am I going to lose next?"

Garrin withdrew his arm and dodged the question. "It'll take time, but you will feel better eventually."

Oracus sighed and wiped the tears from his face. "I hope you're right," he said, unconvinced.

When the grave was filled with earth, the crowd slowly thinned until Oracus was left alone. Soon, the cemetery was empty and silent, with not even the bustle of the markets audible in the distance. Oracus knelt beside the grave and placed his hand on the corner of the gravestone. The feeling comforted him like he was grasping his father's shoulder.

"Thank you for everything," he said simply. He let the

words linger for a moment in the hope his father would respond to him. But when the silence endured, he spoke on, "I promise I'll make you proud."

The tears returned to his eyes again, but this time he didn't hold them back. He let them flow until the afternoon became evening, and then evening became night. When darkness arrived, the air turned cool, but Oracus still didn't leave his father's side. He would stay there until morning, or until all his tears had dried up.

*

Several days passed after the burial and the dull ache of grief and anguish persisted. Only when preoccupied could Oracus prevent the sadness, so he'd often take walks through Afarra's streets with Bandor tucked safely inside his shirt. For the most part, he kept Bandor well hidden, but sometimes the Lion's head would pop out of his collar for a look around and someone would inevitably spot him. On those occasions, Oracus would quickly find the nearest alley or doorway to escape through before a crowd began to gather.

When he wasn't exploring the city, he was usually avoiding Garrin or other villagers of Thessley. For hours, he would lock himself inside the room where his father had died, and either sleep or talk to Bandor. Although dusty, cold and empty, the small room comforted Oracus somewhat – the air in there still carried the scent of his father; or maybe that was just Oracus's imagination.

It had been barely a week since Bandor had appeared in

the Raspian Forest, but already he and Oracus had a bond unlike anything Oracus had ever experienced. When Oracus had taken the Lion back to the barn in Thessley, he had been aware of a connection between them, but now he sensed that Bandor understood every word he spoke, and he even had a suspicion the Lion could read his thoughts.

On a morning when the sky was cloudless and blue above Afarra, Oracus and Bandor were lying together on the floor of their room. They had recently returned from a visit to the cemetery and were having a quiet snooze.

Suddenly, Oracus snapped awake at the sound of a voice. He looked around the room and realised they were still alone. He wondered if he'd been dreaming, and then shook Bandor's peaceful body. "Are you awake?" he whispered.

Bandor's ears twitched and he lifted his head. Then Oracus realised what he had heard.

"You can talk, can't you?" he said to the Lion.

There wasn't an immediate response, but then Bandor's mouth moved and a soft reply came, "Yes."

For a moment, Oracus said nothing, he just looked into Bandor's big yellow eyes. But then a smile spread across his face for the first time since his father had died. "How long have you been able to?" he said.

Bandor blinked and purred quietly. "I don't know. It just feels right today." His voice was so calm and deliberate it instantly relaxed Oracus. It was like listening to the patter of rain on a window.

"I have so many questions to ask you," Oracus said.

"I already know what your questions are," Bandor replied. "But I won't be able to answer them. I know nothing except what I've learned from you."

"So you don't know where you came from or why you landed in the forest?" Oracus pressed.

Bandor shook his feline head. "All I know is my arrival here has forced you out of your home, and I'm sorry for that."

Oracus stood up and walked over to the window. Down below, a bustling market square was full of life. In one corner, a butcher was swinging a cleaver dangerously above his head and hollering about *'the finest cuts of meat in Afarra',* while in another corner, several women were eyeing the gems on a jewellery stall. In the centre of the square, two boys were pushing their way through the crowd to see the swords at the weaponry stall, just like Oracus and Garrin used to do in Thessley when they were younger.

An emptiness filled Oracus as he turned back towards Bandor. What he'd give to be back by the hearth in his home with his father sitting in the rocking chair and blowing smoke-rings at the ceiling. "It's not your fault. I don't blame you," Oracus assured Bandor. "But everything I used to rely on has gone. Even the people from Thessley don't seem the same anymore." Oracus turned his attention back to the market. "I mean, what are we supposed to do here? Is this our home forever now?"

Bandor crept forward and rubbed his head affectionately against Oracus's leg. "Maybe all this is happening for a reason. Maybe we found each other in the forest because it's our destiny to take on the world together."

Oracus looked down at Bandor but withheld his response. Right now, an adventure of some kind was the last thing he wanted.

"I understand," Bandor said. "Nobody expects you to forget about your father or Thessley, but you can't stay in this room forever without speaking to the people you care about."

"I'm not in the mood to talk to anyone," Oracus replied with a shrug. "I don't have anything to say to them."

"At some point you'll have to. They'll come to you if you don't find them first. And don't you want to discover more about Pharia now it's no longer a secret?"

The truth was that Oracus was extremely interested in discovering more about Pharia. For years he had wanted to know the answers that were being kept from him. But it was his curiosity that had got him into this mess in the first place, so he was reluctant to go asking questions in case it made everything worse.

"Why don't we take a walk?" Bandor said. "Being in the sunshine might cheer you up."

Oracus grumbled but peeled his eyes away from the people in the market square. "We could go to the far side of the city and see the ocean. I haven't seen the ocean before."

"Neither have I," Bandor added.

Bandor had grown to twice the size since Oracus had first found him, and Oracus's shirt could no longer contain him. So Oracus manufactured a harness out of the bedsheets and put Bandor inside. When they were both comfortable, they exited the house through the back door and took to the narrow, cobbled lanes outside.

In the backstreets of Afarra, the laughter of children bounced off the stone buildings, and the wonderful smell of cooking meat lingered in the summer air. While the children played, the elderly stood watchfully in porches and doorways, mostly knitting, or smoking, or hanging clothes out to dry in the sun.

After several minutes of walking, the lanes opened out and the yellow stone buildings were replaced by tiny thatched homes with short fences surrounding them and flowers on the windowsills. Outside one of the houses, an old lady was pruning a bush, just like Oracus would have seen in Thessley. The sight made him smile, but sorrow soon followed, and he looked away and quickened his pace.

When the sun had reached its highest point, Oracus and Bandor arrived at a field bestrewn with apple trees. The field was full of joy and laughter, with children flying kites and throwing balls with their parents, while apple-pickers climbed ladders to reach the highest fruits. Beyond the field, Oracus caught his first ever glimpse of the ocean, with its gentle blue waves glimmering with white in the sunlight. The sound of the water crashing onto the sandy shore was even more calming than the trickle of stream water in the forest.

When Oracus stepped onto the field, Bandor's sensitive nose rose out of the sheet harness and sniffed the air. His metal whiskers tickled Oracus's chin.

"This part of the city is beautiful," Oracus observed. "Why didn't we come here sooner?" He walked across the field and between the trees, until his feet sank into the soft sand.

With the water splashing at his feet, Oracus inhaled a deep, peaceful breath and tasted the salt in the air. Then there was a screech from behind, and he turned around to see Garrin and the Eagle soaring over the field towards him.

The Eagle landed with a small hop and ruffled its metal feathers. It snapped its beak several times and Oracus took a surprised step away.

"She won't hurt you," Garrin said as he dropped from the saddle on the Eagle's back. "She just looks fierce."

The Eagle stood a foot taller than Oracus and its sharp eyes had locked onto him. He wasn't convinced it was completely harmless.

"Her name's Aquila," Garrin went on, stroking her neck. "She actually already knows quite a lot about you."

Oracus struggled to take his eyes off Aquila, but when Bandor poked his head out of the harness, Oracus looked down. "This is Bandor," he said.

Garrin stroked Bandor's head and grinned, then his expression turned more serious. "You've been avoiding everyone since the funeral," he said. "Are you okay?"

Oracus shrugged. "I just wanted to be alone for a while."

"I came to see you, but you'd locked yourself away."

"I just wasn't in the mood for visitors, that's all."

Unsurprisingly, the sound of excited voices soon came from all around them. Because of Garrin and Aquila's overt arrival, the peaceful spot on the shore was suddenly being invaded by people wanting to meet them.

Garrin was quick to react and pulled Oracus to Aquila's side. "Get on," he ordered.

Just as they'd done when escaping from Thessley, Oracus and Garrin climbed onto Aquila's back and they took off into the sky. Disappointed shouts reached them, but soon the people were out of sight and a spectacular view of miles and miles of ocean was all Oracus could see.

High above the land was a truly incredible place to be, but it also brought about a frustration in Oracus that he couldn't explain. "Why did you keep all this from me, Garrin?" he asked sternly.

Garrin fidgeted in the saddle behind Oracus. "I wanted to tell you, but I couldn't. I made a promise to say nothing because I thought it would keep Thessley safe."

"But it didn't," Oracus contended. "If anything, your secrets were the reason the soldiers found Thessley. If you'd been honest with me then I would never have been in the forest to find Bandor, and the village would never have been discovered."

"I asked you not to speak to Elnir but you went and did it anyway," Garrin argued. "I tried to warn you."

"You lied to me!"

"I didn't lie," Garrin defended.

"You told me Elnir's stories were nonsense, but you knew they weren't. You tried to convince me this world outside Thessley didn't exist when you were actually a Rider all along." Oracus shook his head. "My best friend became a Rider and didn't even tell me."

"I wish I could have," Garrin said. "Every day I wanted to share it with you."

"But you didn't, and now my father is dead."

Garrin stiffened in his seat at those words. For a short time, he said nothing at all, and Oracus began to feel guilty for being so cutting. He knew Garrin would never have purposely put his father's life in danger, but he had harboured so much anger since leaving Thessley that he'd needed to release it somehow.

When Garrin did eventually speak, each word caught in

his throat. "Do you think I haven't thought about it a thousand times since? I wish I could turn back time and change something, but I can't! I'm sorry, Oracus. I really am."

The view of the ocean became less breathtaking when marred by regret. Oracus ran his fingers through his hair and sighed. "No, it's me who should be sorry, Garrin. I know you didn't mean for this to happen. Blaming you wasn't fair."

Garrin put his hand on Oracus's shoulder. "Shall we forget about our disagreements and start afresh?" he said.

"Only if you now promise to tell me everything you know about Pharia," Oracus replied.

"Well, the leader of this city has been quite keen to meet you since you arrived," Garrin said. "His name is Torvanon and he's a Rider too. How about I take you to meet him?"

Oracus nodded his head. "I think I'd like that."

Following Oracus's approval, Aquila's right wing declined and she arched back towards the city. In the very centre of Afarra, a palace stood tall and magnificent, and the Eagle soared effortlessly towards it.

NINE

Introduction To War

Aquila landed in a huge courtyard full of lush green grass and flowers of every colour imaginable. It was the perfect prelude to the impressive palace that overlooked it, with picnickers lounging on the lawns and soaking up the summer heat. The palace itself was colossal, built to four square tiers of yellow sandstone, with arched windows aplenty. On the parapet of the first tier, archers in green cloaks watched over the grounds below.

As soon as Aquila was noticed by those in the courtyard, a swell of noise arose and a crowd began to amass. Aquila took flight again, leaving Oracus, Garrin and Bandor to fend for themselves, so they quickly marched to the shallow palace steps before the congregation could gather too much momentum. At the top of the steps, two soldiers with spears guarded the heavy oak door, but they stood aside as they were approached. The door swung inwards and offered Oracus, Garrin and Bandor passage inside. What awaited them took Oracus's breath away.

A huge entrance hall with a dozen carved pillars was decorated with fancy green and gold banners. In the centre of the high ceiling, a heavy glass chandelier dangled unlit given the sunlight beaming through the many windows. On the opposite side of the hall, two grand mahogany staircases curved up to a balcony that overlooked the foyer. On the balcony, and all around the walls within the hall, doorways led to other areas of the palace.

There was so much to take in that Oracus was passing through another oak door before he'd had chance to see everything. But if he thought the entrance hall was grandiose, then it was nothing compared to the grand hall that followed. In the grand hall, the walls were decorated with the same green and gold banners, and another thirty or more columns held up a ceiling that was even higher than that in the foyer. The floor beneath a dozen long feast tables was of cobbled grey stone that was dressed in a royal green rug that ran the whole length of the room. And in niches all around the walls, marble soldiers with their weapons drawn posed impressively on white podiums.

Garrin led Oracus and Bandor to the far side of the hall, where a large man wearing armour and a golden cloak was sat in a throne. Beside the throne, a Lavorian far larger than any creature Oracus had seen before lay with its eyes closed; it was so still it could have passed for a huge pile of silver coins.

"Welcome, guests!" the man bellowed so loudly that his voice ricocheted off the walls. He stood from his throne and bounded towards them, the green gems in his chestplate shining brightly in the light. "Welcome to my city!"

"This is Torvanon," Garrin said quietly to Oracus as the man approached.

Torvanon seemed to get bigger the closer he came. He was about the size of Karvan, the fight trainer from Thessley, with broad shoulders and a barrel chest, both accentuated by his thick armour. The hair on his head and face was as orange as you'll see, and his red face was full of joy.

Oracus held out a hand to greet Torvanon, but his hand was swatted away and he was grasped in a hug that lifted him off his feet.

"It's nice to finally meet you, Oracus," Torvanon said. "And to meet you too…" He looked down at the Lion in Oracus's harness, and then to Oracus for assistance.

"Bandor," Oracus clarified.

"… Bandor!" Torvanon finished. And with a gentle hand for such a big man, patted Bandor on the head. "I'm sorry you had to leave your village in such a hurry," Torvanon went on. "And I'm especially sorry that you lost your father. I trust you've had time to mourn?"

Oracus nodded his head meekly. "Thank you for letting us stay here," he said.

Torvanon waved his hands dismissively. "The pleasure is all mine. Here, come and meet Ursus. He's much softer than he appears, please don't be intimidated."

The giant pile of silver beside the throne stirred and rose to its feet. Oracus gulped as he looked up at a Bear Lavorian about three times his height, with a head as large as a cart. All over its body, the silver metal armour was of fur just like Bandor's, but its claws were all like curved swords that scratched against the stone floor. The Bear just planting its feet beneath itself made the whole room tremble.

Ursus opened his mouth and spoke in a voice as deep as you'd expect from a creature his size, "Welcome to Afarra," he said.

Oracus just gaped at the Lavorian and struggled to speak. He was glad Ursus didn't give hugs to newcomers like his Rider did.

Torvanon took to his throne again, and Ursus dropped back onto his belly and rested his colossal head on his paws. Oracus thought he heard the floor crack.

"It's been many years since there have been three Lavorians in this city," Torvanon said happily. "It makes me feel young again."

Oracus watched Torvanon closely and considered his age. "You don't look particularly old though," he observed.

Torvanon appeared amused. "Being a Rider keeps me looking young. Trust me, I am much older than you think." He clasped his fingers together and leaned forwards. "Anyway, Oracus, let's cut to the chase. Tell me how you and Bandor first met."

The question took Oracus aback. When Garrin had suggested meeting the leader of Afarra, he hadn't expected it to be someone like Torvanon. He had prepared himself for someone very serious and insensitive, not a man so friendly and courteous. "Well, I was taking a walk in the forest at night," he started. Then he went on to explain how the forest had felt unusually eerie, how the rock had fallen from the sky, and how he had carried Bandor back to Thessley during a thunderstorm. He told Torvanon how he'd found soldiers in the forest the following day whilst hunting, and how Garrin and Aquila had saved his life. "And then they brought Bandor and I back here," he ended.

"Coincidentally, I bonded with Ursus during a stormy night in the Raspian Forest too," Torvanon claimed. He appeared to reminisce for a moment and the corners of his mouth twitched behind his auburn beard. "We've been companions for almost sixty years. He was Bandor's size at first. I could pick him up and we would sleep in the same bed together. Oh, how things change – now he would squash me by sitting on me!"

"Sixty years?" Oracus repeated. "How is that possible? You look no older than fifty!"

Torvanon laughed this time. "As I said before, I do not age. Riders don't! Many years ago, before war ruined this land, there were Riders who were hundreds of years old, and their Lavorians were far larger than you would dare to imagine."

"So the three of us will never die?" Oracus said.

"Not unless we are killed," Torvanon replied with a nonchalant shrug.

Oracus wasn't sure he liked the idea of living forever, and he decided not to think about it. "What happened to those Riders and Lavorians?" he asked instead. "Did they die during the war?"

"The infamous Noble War," Torvanon said with a sigh. "It all happened long before even I was born. Every Rider was killed in that war, and every Lavorian destroyed. And still to this day we don't know how or why."

Oracus was suddenly reminded of how little he knew about Pharia and its history. Since he had been forced to leave Thessley, he had been bombarded with new information and experiences, and he was feeling increasingly overwhelmed.

"But Riders and Lavorians are back, and we have another war to prepare for," Torvanon said.

"A war against King Jowra?" Oracus asked, thinking back to Elnir's story in the Old Mill Inn.

Torvanon gave him a sharp look. "You know of Jowra?"

"I only heard about him recently," Oracus replied. "Nobody really knew anything about this land back in Thessley."

Garrin shuffled uncomfortably beside Oracus and looked up at the ceiling.

"Well, King Jowra is indeed who we are going to war against," Torvanon clarified. "He's somewhat of a dictator."

"Why are you intent on fighting him and not joining him?" Oracus asked.

"Because I believe there is a balance that should be maintained within Pharia. After the Noble War, when Riders and Lavorians were gone, every race in the land united. For years, the balance was kept intact. But fast-forward two centuries to when the Riders and Lavorians returned, and suddenly there's power to be gained and the balance is inevitably lost." Torvanon's red face had sagged into a scowl. "Jowra is a man seeking power. He's attempting to control all Pharia's realms to stop anyone from challenging his reign. He wants to be King forever."

"But even with Jowra dead, there will still be Riders and Lavorians here to seek power," Oracus argued. "Or do you plan to kill them all?"

"Jowra believes being a Rider gives him the right to control the land," Torvanon explained. "But if we win this war, I would ensure we use our power to protect Pharia, not to dominate the many people who live here."

Oracus had already felt the effects of Jowra's rule when his father had died, so he was all for the King being stopped. But Torvanon was speaking to him like he would have some influence in Jowra's downfall. He was just a young man from a small village who happened to find a Lavorian in the forest. It had only been a week ago that four soldiers had almost killed him in a field. "I don't really know what you expect of me though," he aired.

"Killing Jowra before he kills us is the only way to stop him," Torvanon said. "An extra Rider will help us achieve that, and it will boost the morale of the soldiers. You've already seen how the people in the city react to you."

"You don't expect me to fight in this war, do you?"

"Not today. But you'll be ready when your training is complete. You may just be the difference between victory and failure."

"Training?" Oracus blurted. "What training?"

"There's no way you'd be capable of killing Jowra without training to be an effective Rider," Torvanon said. "He's the strongest Rider in the land. I'm not sure it's possible to kill him even with training!"

Oracus was beginning to get a familiar feeling of dread. When he had listened to Elnir's story he had felt a similar emotion. People talked about Jowra in a way that made him feel uneasy; it left a strange taste in his mouth.

"Honestly, Oracus, it's a pleasure to have you here in Afarra!" Torvanon clapped his hands together and stood up from his throne. "There has been a vacant room here in the palace since you arrived. I understand you haven't used it yet. I'm sure Garrin will happily lead you to it now. Do you have any questions before you leave?"

Oracus was wondering how he had found himself in such a predicament. But he was so bemused he just shook his head at Torvanon. In the last hour, he had been drawn into a war that he knew nothing about, except that it would probably end up killing him.

"You'd better get some rest," Torvanon said as he clasped Oracus in another rib-cracking hug. "Your training begins tomorrow. And it will be tough. Very tough!"

TEN

Lavorian In Mind

Oracus found himself face to face with Garrin under the shadow of the palace the next morning. It was early, and the air was still cool, but it was to be a sunny day in Afarra once again.

They occupied the gravel sparring area to the rear of the palace, which was long and thin, with several archery targets to one side. It was better maintained than the training area in Thessley, as you would expect, but it was far less busy. It seemed the soldiers of Afarra didn't do their training at dawn; so Oracus and Garrin were alone.

Oracus was stood in the green leather armour he had taken from the armoury, and he also had a lightweight helmet perched on his head. Garrin mirrored him, and they both held a silver sword in their hands with a plain golden handle.

"Should I assume now that I'm actually much worse at sword fighting than you?" Oracus asked. "It would be naïve of me to think the Garrin I sparred with in Thessley a few days ago was the real Garrin. I've seen you kill a man since."

Garrin smiled knowingly. "I won't let you off as lightly as I did before. You're a good swordsman though, Oracus. That much is clear."

Oracus attempted to prove Garrin right and charged with his sword raised, determined to catch his friend off-guard. He swung for the head, but Garrin deflected the strike and retaliated with a blow that knocked Oracus to the ground.

"You're better than that," Garrin said simply, and he gestured for Oracus to get back to his feet.

When he was ready, Oracus tried again to defeat his opponent quickly. He thrust at Garrin and tried to stab his chest, but the attack was dodged and Oracus found himself on his back again.

He remained recumbent for a moment to regain some of the air that had been knocked out his lungs. When he got up, he decided being smarter with his attacks might be the best way to outwit Garrin. He raised his sword until the hilt was level with his face, then he feigned to strike Garrin's left, but instead, turned and swung at his right shoulder. Garrin cleverly anticipated the move, ducked under Oracus's sword and swiped his legs from beneath him. For the third time, Oracus hit the floor hard.

The humiliation of defeat endured for a further half hour. Oracus would repeatedly get up, attack Garrin, and then find himself on the ground, or on the end of a painful strike to his torso.

"I can't do this anymore," he wheezed from the floor, through deep breaths of exhaustion and pain. "You're faster than I am, and you seem to know what I'm going to do before even I do. I haven't struck you once and you've hit me a hundred times."

"You're predictable," Garrin said simply. "You always attack me first; you never wait for me to make the initial move. And when you attack, your eyes give away your intentions every time. You look at the part of my body you're planning to strike."

"You're saying I don't know how to use a sword?" Oracus assumed unhappily.

"No, you're actually very good with a sword. It's your brain that needs practise." Garrin prodded his temple with a finger. "Come on, let's try again."

Reluctantly, Oracus agreed and faced Garrin. Looking at Garrin's armour, he could see barely a mark on it, but his own was covered in dents and scratches. He focused his mind and decided this time he would wait for Garrin to make the first move. When Garrin did eventually strike, Oracus was fast enough to deflect the blow. Garrin staggered backwards and grimaced, then launched himself at Oracus again and swung his sword several times at Oracus's body. Oracus blocked each of the attacks with his sword but Garrin was fast and his strikes fierce. They stepped apart for a second, and Oracus took the time to inhale a deep breath. But Garrin was quick to take advantage and charged his shoulder into Oracus's chest. Oracus fell backwards and gasped as the gravel floor peeled the skin off the palms of his hands.

"That was better," Garrin praised. "You made me work for that."

*

In the meadow adjacent to the sparring area, just out of

Oracus and Garrin's view, Bandor was stood with Aquila. It was calm and peaceful except for the occasional sound of clashing swords beyond the long grass, and there was barely a breeze to ripple the tops of the pines in the nearby woodland. The clouds were yet again scarce above Afarra, and the morning air was beginning to warm. Sunlight beamed across the meadow, and the flowers offered fragrant aromas that nestled unpleasantly in Bandor's sensitive nose.

Bandor was with Aquila, as Oracus was with Garrin, to train. But Bandor wasn't being trained to kill or fight – he was already programmed to be very effective at that. In fact, he was required to learn the skills needed by a Lavorian during battle. As Aquila had wisely said, *'A Lavorian should instinctively put its Rider's life before its own. But a skilled Lavorian would always intervene before a sacrifice became necessary.'* And to do that, a Lavorian must understand its Rider's mind, and foresee its Rider's intentions.

"I often know what Oracus is thinking," Bandor explained. "And I can usually sense his emotions too."

"That's part of a Rider and Lavorian's bond," Aquila replied. "I can read Garrin's thoughts. And I see what he sees, hear what he hears, and taste what he tastes. Over time, you will learn to do this with Oracus, but it takes a lot of practise to develop."

"How do I do it?" Bandor enquired.

"Well, the greater the distance between you and Oracus, the harder it will be to connect to his mind," Aquila explained. "But whenever you are close, and you sense his mind is accessible, you must delve into it. The more you enter his mind now, the stronger your bond will become in the future."

Bandor attempted to link his mind with Oracus's, but he could feel nothing this morning. Their usual bond seemed to be missing. "I don't feel anything today," he said.

"Let's get closer to the sparring area," Aquila suggested. "Maybe the distance is too much."

Together, they proceeded towards the edge of the meadow, carving a path through the long grass. Nearer the sparring area, the clanging of swords became louder.

"Any better?" Aquila said.

It was, and Bandor nodded. With Oracus now in sight, their minds had joined. And notably, Bandor could feel a frustration within his Rider.

"See if you can go deeper," Aquila urged.

Bandor did as Aquila suggested and closed his eyes to help his concentration. At first, he didn't know what he was searching for. But then he became drawn to something that intrigued him. Following his intuition, he reached further into Oracus's mind, but it was like trying to grasp something slippery. Yet after several failed attempts, he finally clutched the feeling and pulled himself in.

Bandor's immediate reaction was of surprise. Then the dull aching pain came. He opened his eyes and saw Garrin was stood over him. He was lying on his back on the gravel, feeling exhausted and hurt. They were under the shadow of the palace, and his sword was free of his hand. He had been defeated.

Bandor's vision faltered and he lost his focus. He was stood once again in the meadow with Aquila, and thankfully, the pain in his body had already eased.

*

Oracus lay on his back feeling exhausted and hurt. Garrin stood over him with his sword in his hand and a grin on his face. Oracus's sword had escaped his grasp and lay abandoned in the gravel several feet away, and his armour was in a state beyond repair.

When Oracus had fallen for what must have been the thousandth time, he'd felt a strange sensation in his mind. Passing it off as a result of too many blows to the head, he climbed gingerly back to his feet and prepared for Garrin's next onslaught.

"No, that'll do for today," Garrin said, much to Oracus's relief. "Why don't we take a seat for a minute? I have something to show you."

With his curiosity piqued, Oracus found the strength to follow Garrin to a wooden table beside the sparring area. Garrin picked up a stone from the ground, placed it on the table and sat. Oracus dropped heavily into the seat opposite and tried not to focus on his aching muscles.

"The quirks of being a Rider are not just the Lavorian they bond with and the improved fighting skills they acquire," Garrin said. "They also gain a superpower. For example, I can manipulate earth and water with my mind." As he spoke, the stone on the table rose into the air and floated at eye level. Then it wobbled and dropped back onto the table with a clunk.

Oracus let out a gasp of shock. "How did you do that?"

Garrin laughed. "Do you want me to show you again?" This time, the stone lifted off the table and launched itself across the sparring area as if Garrin had thrown it with his hand.

"That's incredible!" Oracus exclaimed, his eyes wide with fascination.

"All Riders have a power, Oracus."

"You mean I can move stones with my mind too?" Oracus said, pointing at himself.

"You can't move stones, no," Garrin answered. "Every Rider's power is unique. No two are the same."

"Then how do I find out what mine is?" Oracus asked without hesitation.

"Patience," Garrin said. "I discovered mine when I was angry one day. I accidentally hit Aquila in the face with a rock."

"So I need to get angry?"

"No, you need to wait. It will show itself when the time is right."

Oracus bit his lip and strummed his fingers on his knee. He looked at another stone on the floor and tried to move it with a powerful stare. Nothing happened. "What's Torvanon's power?" he asked suddenly.

"He can manipulate metal with his mind. He's been a Rider for decades so can do some amazing things."

"Do you mean powers get stronger over time?"

"It's practising that makes them stronger. It's like building a muscle, I guess."

Oracus felt a pang of glee. Followed by a stab of doubt. The thought of having a power was exciting, but what if his power turned out to be boring and useless? Surely if it was so great he'd have noticed it by now.

"Is everything okay?" Garrin asked him. "You look

puzzled."

Oracus was midway through nodding when he felt that same odd feeling in his head again, like someone was meddling with his brain. He shook his head and tried to force the sensation away, but it persisted until he heard a voice.

"Hello, Oracus," it said.

It wasn't through his ears that Oracus heard Bandor, it was more like a direct connection to his brain. It was the most peculiar feeling he had ever experienced.

"Humans see things much differently to Lavorians," Bandor observed.

"You can see what I'm seeing?" Oracus replied, speaking somehow through his mind and not his mouth.

"I can, but the colours are very dull!" Bandor said. *"It feels like night."*

"How did you get into my mind?"

"Aquila taught me," Bandor said. *"But it's really hard to concentrate–"*

Oracus lost contact with Bandor and squinted to refocus his eyes on what was around him. He was surprised to find Garrin staring at him.

"Bandor?" his friend asked with a smile.

"How do you know that?" Oracus answered.

"Because your eyes glazed over and you weren't listening to a word I was saying."

"Oh, sorry. I didn't hear you."

"Don't apologise," Garrin said. "It was eight weeks before Aquila and I could link our minds. You've found yourself a strong Lavorian, Oracus."

*

Bandor shook himself and his metal fur jingled quietly. He had successfully connected with Oracus's mind, but it had taken a lot of effort to do so.

"Why did that drain so much of my energy?" he asked, dropping onto his belly in the long grass.

"Why does it cost so much energy to run a long distance?" Aquila said. "Simply because you're doing something your body isn't used to. You're still quite a distance from Oracus too, that's no easy feat."

"Tell me it gets easier," Bandor prompted, panting slightly.

"With practise," Aquila assured.

Bandor put his head on his paws and closed his eyes. "We see things a lot differently," he said.

"Our senses are stronger than a Human's," Aquila agreed. "And our Riders will rely on them in dangerous situations."

"Do we always feel their pain when we enter their minds too?"

"If Oracus is feeling pain, then you will feel it too," Aquila explained. "But a more experienced Lavorian can enter his Rider's mind without feeling pain, or he can project the pain entirely upon himself so his Rider isn't disadvantaged in a fight." Aquila ruffled her metal feathers and snapped her beak. "I've heard a Lavorian with ultimate control can totally eradicate pain in himself *and* his Rider – but it's so difficult to accomplish I'm not even sure the mighty King Jowra can do it."

Bandor lifted his head and looked through the shoots of

grass towards the sparring area. He couldn't wait until he was strong enough to take Oracus's pain away from him, even if he had to endure it himself. Maybe by then, he would be able to enter Oracus's mind without it being so exhausting too.

After a moment, Aquila unfolded her wings and stretched them out. "Garrin and Oracus are done," she said as she flapped them gently. "You can go and get some rest now."

Bandor yawned as he got to his feet, and along with Aquila, he waded through the grass towards where Oracus and Garrin were waiting.

ELEVEN

Guests From Tallarin

After they finished training in the morning, Oracus rested and bathed in his new room in the palace until evening arrived. Then, accompanied by Bandor, he navigated his way along corridors and down staircases to the grand hall. It was time for the evening feast, and when Oracus arrived in the hall, he was received by tumultuous applause from the many soldiers who filled the long tables.

After being shocked by the warmth of his welcome, Oracus was ushered to the top-table where Torvanon, Garrin and another man were sat. The three of them each had a goblet of wine in their hand and a plate of food on the table in front of them.

Torvanon poured wine into a fourth goblet and gave it to Oracus as he approached. "They love you already!" he said happily of the soldiers who were staring up at Oracus and the top-table. "Alright now!" he bellowed loudly to them. "Back to your meals."

When Oracus took a seat at the table, Garrin offered him a smile. "I hope you're not hurting too much from practise earlier," he said with a sly wink.

Oracus scowled. "I'm covered from head to toe in bruises," he complained quietly.

"Oracus, I would like to introduce you to Horvos," Torvanon said, gesturing to the third man at the table. "Commander of Afarra's soldiers."

Horvos was the same size as Torvanon, with both a barrel chest and broad shoulders. But his hair and beard were grey and wiry, and his skin weathered and dark. He wore metal gauntlets on his arms and a plate across his chest, as if convinced a battle was likely to break out during the feast. He gripped Oracus's hand firmly and nodded his head once.

"It's great to meet you," Oracus returned.

Within seconds of Oracus sitting, a huge plate of food had been placed in front of him. He took a sip of his wine, and began to eat with his hands, tearing pig meat off the bone with his teeth.

"This reminds me of the day you arrived, Garrin," Torvanon said with a loud guffaw. "Have you told Oracus what you first thought of Ursus?"

Garrin's cheeks turned pink when he faced Oracus. "I was warned Ursus devoured anyone who looked him in the eye, and I believed it," he said.

Torvanon laughed louder still. "Every time Garrin walked by, Ursus snapped his jaws and Garrin would run!"

"It took a whole month for me to realise it was a joke," Garrin added. "I was terrified."

Oracus ate until his belly was full, drank until his head was spinning, and laughed until his cheeks hurt. For the whole evening, Bandor slept soundly on his knee. Only when the early hours of the morning came did he bid his farewells and retire to his room.

Once undressed and lying on his bed, Oracus was able to relax, and he felt for the first time he could learn to like Afarra. He missed Thessley greatly, but at least the people in Afarra were kind and welcoming. And it was clear there was much more to do and see in a city so vast, rather than a village so small.

Looking at the patterned ceiling above through drunken eyes and darkness, Oracus's attention turned to his connection with Bandor. If the Lavorian hadn't been by his side then he'd have been far less accepting of the transition from Thessley to Afarra. And since the Lion had broken into his mind during training with Garrin earlier in the day, he had felt especially close to him. There was an even greater trust and respect between them.

"How did you enter my mind at the sparring area?" Oracus asked aloud.

"I'm not sure," Bandor replied. "I could just feel your presence and I forced my way in."

As they were speaking, Oracus could feel a strange presence in his own head; in fact, he'd felt it for most of the day. It was an unusual tingling sensation behind his eyes. By now, he had assumed it was Bandor's mind, and he was eager to enter it.

"Go ahead," Bandor offered, predicting Oracus's intentions.

Oracus focused his inebriated mind and closed his eyes. It took several seconds, but suddenly his concentration peaked, and he slipped into Bandor's head.

The room that had been dark only seconds before, suddenly became as bright as if it were daytime. The ceiling above was full of colour, and the thin drapes hanging from the posts of the bed were as golden as sunlight. There was a babble of voices from other rooms in the palace that Oracus hadn't noticed before, and he even spotted the movement of a tiny moth outside the window. Compared to his own senses, Bandor's were incredible. The Lion was so attuned, in fact, that Oracus struggled to maintain his focus. And as quickly as he had fallen into Bandor's mind, he fell back out, and was once again consumed by darkness. Instantly, the last of his energy was drained from his body, and he plunged into the deepest of sleeps.

*

As was to be routine for the foreseeable future, Oracus and Bandor made their way to the sparring area at the break of dawn the next morning. Daylight was beginning to creep over the pines in the woodland, but the sparring area was still cast in shadow.

Oracus was unsure how he'd cope with another day like the one before. His muscles were sore, and he was unimpressed with having to wake up so early. But when he and Bandor approached the sparring area, there was a small crowd of soldiers gathered in a circle, and they were cheering two men who were sparring quite ferociously.

With Bandor in his arms, Oracus squeezed through the audience and saw the two fighters were Garrin and Torvanon. Garrin in his green leather, and Torvanon wearing majestic golden armour. Against Torvanon, Garrin looked small and weak, and he was beginning to hide under his wooden shield, while Torvanon was trying to smash through it with a heavy axe. For a worrying moment, Oracus thought Torvanon might chop Garrin in half, but Torvanon relented for just a second and gave Garrin enough time to escape. Garrin staggered away from his stronger foe and discarded his broken shield, and then the two men faced each other for their final assault.

There was a glint in Torvanon's eyes now, and he looked confident. Garrin, on the other hand, already looked defeated.

"This is it, Garrin," Torvanon provoked. "It's your chance!"

Torvanon raised his axe and charged forwards. Garrin braced himself, and then a clump of loose gravel rose from the ground and struck Torvanon in the face. The leader of Afarra came to a halt and began to cough heavily, and then more gravel was flung at him until his bushy beard and eyebrows were full of dust.

"Your power is getting stronger, but it's not strong enough," Torvanon said hoarsely. He raised a hand and wrenched Garrin's sword out of his grasp with his own power, and then used the sword to pin Garrin to the ground.

"He can manipulate metal," Bandor said inside Oracus's mind.

Garrin struggled against the sword momentarily, which Torvanon still held firmly in place with his power, and then went limp.

"I concede," he said. "You're far too strong."

The audience burst into applause and Torvanon bowed proudly to them all. He offered a deep booming laugh, and then released the sword.

"I could have carved you into a sculpture with your own weapon," he said playfully. "Imagine that!" It was then that Torvanon noticed Oracus in the crowd. He offered a broad smile and spread his arms wide in greeting. "You saw me defeat your friend," he said.

Oracus nodded. "It was really impressive."

Torvanon's expression of triumph eased slightly. "Well, I have had more than half a century of practise. You both have quite a lot of catching up to do." He shrugged and then twirled his beard with a finger. "But I didn't come here this morning to train. I came to inform you and Garrin that a meeting is due to take place. Messengers have arrived from across the land and I need you both to be there."

"You want me?" Oracus asked, surprised.

"You're a Rider, so your involvement is important," Torvanon explained. "The meeting will start within the hour. I'll see you in the council room."

*

Instead of spending his morning being tortured by Garrin, Oracus found himself sat at a round table in a room at the back of the palace. The council room was a tiny, windowless box that would struggle to fit a dozen people inside. It was cramped and stuffy, and it carried a similar aroma to that of the flowers in the meadow outside. On two of the walls, oil lamps offered a dim orange glow in the darkness.

When Oracus and Bandor arrived with Garrin, they were

met by Torvanon and Horvos, as well as two other people that Oracus didn't recognise, who were both of a similar age to him.

"Oracus, Garrin," Torvanon said. "Meet Kivali and Quent from the city of Tallarin. They're here to warn us of increased activity from the King's soldiers."

"Nice to meet you both," Kivali said quickly. She was dark-haired with flawless skin and blue eyes that glowed warmly. She turned her attention back to Torvanon. "There have been scouts observing Tallarin from afar. We think an attack is imminent."

Quent stood up from his seat. He was almost half-a-foot taller than Oracus but looked like he needed a good meal. His limbs were long and gangly, and his red ears stuck out quite noticeably. "It has taken us weeks to get here when it usually takes days," he said in a hostile tone that Oracus didn't like. "King Jowra's soldiers are camped all over the land and their patrols are on all the main routes."

"We've seen no more activity than usual here," Torvanon advised. "A few groups of scouts have been spotted, that's all."

Horvos cleared his throat. "If Jowra was to send his armies to Tallarin now he wouldn't be triumphant. He doesn't have enough troops."

"Who says so?" Quent replied sharply.

"We send scouts to his cities too," Horvos countered. "We have a fair idea how many soldiers he has."

"And you would like to gamble he doesn't have soldiers fighting for him that you don't know about?" Quent pressed. "He does control most of the land and its people, after all."

Horvos stood. "I am confident our scouts have passed us accurate information," he said forcefully.

Torvanon held up a hand and Horvos took his seat again. "I think we can safely assume Jowra doesn't have the strength to invade both Afarra and Tallarin, otherwise he would have done so already." He was far more serious now than Oracus had seen him before. "However, we must treat this adequately and ensure there is a plan in place. Catania would not have sent two messengers to the other side of Pharia if she wasn't concerned."

Oracus's attention was suddenly piqued. The name *Catania* wasn't new to him. A lady with the same name had been in his dreams recently. "Sorry, but who is Catania?" he enquired.

Quent shot him a stern glare. "The Princess of Tallarin, obviously," he snapped. "Our leader."

Oracus scowled at Quent, but then tried to remember his dreams. In one, Catania had been chased through a forest by the King's soldiers. And in another, she had been locked away in a dungeon by the King himself. He wondered what the real Catania looked like, and if she resembled the blonde lady he had seen in his dreams.

"Catania is readying Tallarin's defences," Kivali continued. "The blacksmiths are already forging armour and weapons so every man in the city can fight should they need to."

"She has sent us here to urge you to do the same," Quent said.

The small room fell quiet while Torvanon deliberated what he had been told. To Oracus, it seemed Pharia was in a much more volatile state than he had first thought, and

Jowra may attack at any moment. But if the King did send his forces to Afarra, was Torvanon sufficiently prepared to resist them?

Garrin put his hand in the air to draw everyone's attention. "Can I suggest something?" he asked.

"Go ahead," Torvanon granted.

"We should attack Jowra before he attacks us."

Quent was quick to reject the idea. "That would be playing into his hands. We'll just be sending our troops to slaughter."

"Quent's right," Torvanon agreed. "Our men would be safer behind our walls. We would kill more of Jowra's men if he attacked us."

"But he may not be planning to attack us yet," Garrin argued.

"It'll happen eventually," Kivali said.

"But whenever it is, it'll be on Jowra's terms," Garrin stated. "It will only ever be when he feels he has the highest chance of success."

"The boy has a point," Horvos said with a nod.

"I'm not saying we should march right into his palace in Melzor and kill him," Garrin explained. "We should focus instead on the other cities he controls elsewhere in the land. Fervia, Lalacia, Alvoria, Malum; any of those could work."

"Taking a handful of soldiers isn't going to be enough to invade any of King Jowra's cities!" Quent declared hotly.

Garrin rounded on Quent. "I'm not talking about just sending men there and hoping we can win," he said. "We need to scout each city and then send a force capable of destroying it. Even if we only destroy one city, at least it weakens Jowra."

"We would need to make sure Afarra is still sufficiently defended, just in case Jowra did send an attack," Horvos added.

"This plan would be a huge risk," Quent stated unhappily. "Princess Catania suggested nothing of the sort, and I doubt she would agree to it."

"What do you think, Kivali?" Torvanon asked.

"Well, it's certainly an option," Kivali began, but then her voice tailed off…

Since hearing Catania's name, Oracus had struggled to maintain his focus. The sultry, airless room was making him tired and queasy, and he wished he had a goblet of water to sip from. He shook his head to try and rid some of the lethargy, but succeeded only in making himself feel dizzy. Somewhere just beyond his consciousness, there was a discussion about fighting Jowra; they were considering sending soldiers to destroy his cities around Pharia. But Oracus was more concerned about Catania, and whether his dreams of her had any hint of truth about them. Could he possibly be having visions of Tallarin's leader?

The air in the room became hotter still, and perspiration began to gather on Oracus's face. Within his mind, he could feel Bandor, but he could also sense another nearby presence. He concentrated on that presence and found himself able to connect with it. Suddenly, a metal goblet on the table threw itself at the wall and made a clang that wrenched Oracus from his reverie. Everyone in the room jumped with fright and then there was silence.

Horvos looked at Torvanon, unimpressed. "What did you do that for?" he growled.

"It wasn't me," Torvanon replied. He looked curiously at

the goblet on the floor. "I think Oracus just discovered his power."

TWELVE

A Lavorian Without Its Armour

The sun beamed down from above and zapped the little energy Catania still had left in her body. The yellow desert and blue sky met on a hazy horizon, and the warmth of the sand was almost unbearable. Catania's skin was exposed and burnt, she wore only a rag that was thin and frayed, and the wounds on her wrists and ankles were sore and full of sand. Beneath her, Alticon limped feebly over the desert and panted for water.

Catania ran her hands through Alticon's usually silky fur, but it was rough and brittle, with dirt matting it into clumps. She had her head resting on his back, and she could feel the scattered rhythm of his heart beating under his skin. She thought back to when Alticon had been a Lavorian. Then, he would have raced through the desert and made it back to Tallarin before nightfall. But now he was weak and vulnerable, Jowra's experiments many years before having taken their toll on his body. Now he was without armour and pride, and he was a mere shell of the incredible Wolf he had once been.

Catania and Alticon had been free of Melzor for two

days. Catania's sadistic father, the notorious King Jowra, had forced her to return to Tallarin under his own supervision. Unfortunately, his leverage had been considerable, and Catania had had no choice but to accept his ingenius plan. Her father was in her head now, and he would control her reign from within her. And if she failed to fulfil his demands, he would force her to kill Alticon herself, or destroy her city from the inside with his powers.

A scolding breeze crossed Catania and Alticon's path and thrust yet more sand into Catania's wounds. She'd have cried out in pain if her throat wasn't so dry, but no more than a croak was heard. For most of their time on the sand, confused thoughts whirred in Catania's mind. She had visions of Tallarin and the mountains surrounding it, and she dreamt of the ocean beyond. She thought of her quarters in the palace, and of the men and women who served her so willingly. And then she wondered if it would be for the best for her to die before ever making it back to Tallarin. It would be a shame not to see her home again, but at least her father would no longer be able to use her.

For hours more, the worries persisted. It was the toughest time of Catania's life. It was even more torturous than being shackled in the dungeon. But eventually, the slow tempo of Alticon's steps became too much and Catania fell into a repose. For a short time, peace came to her, and all her concerns were forgotten.

*

The burning sunlight made way for bitter darkness. The temperature had plummeted, and all that was keeping

Catania warm was the heat of Alticon's body underneath her. She shivered from the cold and opened her eyes. Above, thousands of stars twinkled on a cloudless night, and the moon cast light upon the sand, turning it white as chalk.

It was coming to the third day of travelling, and Alticon hadn't stopped for a moment's rest. Neither of them had eaten or drank since before Catania's imprisonment, and every step for Alticon was so strenuous they were barely making any progress at all.

Finally, Catania could stand to see her Wolf suffer no longer. She patted him softly on the back and whispered hoarsely in his ear, "Alticon, stop. You need to rest."

With a defeated sigh, Alticon adhered to her demand and dropped onto his belly. Catania rolled from his back and curled up between his giant paws. In seconds, his eyes had rolled to the back of his head and wheezing snores were coming from his jaws. He was so brave, but exhausted too, and Catania was angry with herself for allowing him to carry her for so long without stopping. A Lavorian lives to protect its Rider, but Alticon was no longer a Lavorian, and therefore unable to act like he once could. He needed food, water and sleep now, and if he didn't get any, he would die.

*

When Catania awoke next, clouds had obscured the moon and the darkness was considerably thicker. She was still partially wrapped in Alticon's white fur, but the flesh that was exposed to the night was terribly cold. For a brief moment, she wished for the midday sun to be blistering her skin again.

From a distance, a howl cut through the night, and during the eerie silence that followed, Catania found herself searching for movement nearby. For a while, there was nothing more to grab her attention, but just as she began to think she was safe, more howls echoed, closer now, and the white eyes of several wolves came out of the darkness.

Catania stiffened in fright as the wolves approached. They were fierce and hungry, with snarled lips showing lots of sharp teeth.

"Alticon!" Catania whispered urgently, ruffling her Wolf's fur with her hand. "Wake up!"

But Alticon slept on, and the pack of wolves edged ever nearer. Catania counted six of them, and they had formed an arch around them in preparation for an attack.

"Alticon! Wake Up!" Catania hissed.

She pulled hard at her Wolf's damaged fur, and that wrenched him from his sleep. He growled loudly at the pain, and then stood quickly to face their enemies. He stepped in front of Catania to separate her from the danger, and then offered a howl of his own to the night.

Alticon was twice the size of the wolves who opposed him, but they could sense his vulnerability. He was unsteady on his legs, and they had strength in numbers. One of the wolves took an opportunity to strike and snapped its jaws at Alticon's face, but the swipe of a heavy paw sent it retreating to its pack.

Another of the wolves pounced, and Alticon held his ground again. But this time, one of his legs buckled and the pack attacked as one.

Suddenly, jaws were snapping and whines of pain were echoing across the desert. But for a blur of sand and fur, Catania could see nothing, and she could do nothing but scream and fear for Alticon's life. She was too weak and scared to interfere, and the fight seemed to go on for hours. But eventually, the pack of wolves scattered into the darkness and Alticon howled again.

As soon as the wolves had left, Alticon fell onto his side and Catania crawled to him.

"Are you okay?" she whispered helplessly.

His flesh was lacerated from head to tail, and his fur was wet with blood. He groaned in pain and struggled to focus his eyes on Catania's.

"You were so brave," she told him. "Thank you."

Alticon closed his eyes and Catania cradled his head. She forgot temporarily about the pain in her own body and focused entirely on the pain in her heart. This wasn't the first time Alticon had saved her life, it had happened numerous times before. But she didn't deserve his loyalty. Those many years ago in the palace in Melzor, she had allowed her father to experiment on Alticon when he had been a Lavorian. She hadn't tried hard enough to stop it, even as his Rider she had been too frightened to intervene. And after months of his torture, they were eventually stripped of their bond, and Alticon was forced to live as an ordinary Wolf. But even in his weakened state, he still fought to protect her. He would endure torture for her, he would walk through scolding deserts for her, and he would fight off anything that would threaten to harm her. After everything she had put him through, he still considered himself to be her Lavorian.

*

When Catania next opened her eyes, the terrifying darkness was gone and the intolerable heat had returned. She was still beside Alticon, and she was relieved to see his chest rising and falling, but horrific patches of scarlet were covering his white coat.

Catania lifted her head to observe her surroundings and was surprised to learn they were on the move. Together, she and Alticon were lying on a wooden board that was being carried by several strange men wearing brown tunics.

Aware the men could be either friend or foe, Catania dropped her head again and tried to keep still, but her movements had already been detected by a young freckly boy no older than twelve.

"Princess!" he shouted in a strange accent. "Yer awake!"

In the time it took for Catania to raise her head again, she and Alticon had been lowered to the ground. The men who had been carrying them gathered around curiously.

"Hello," she muttered nervously.

"It's nice ter meet yer acquaintance, Ma'am," one of the men replied with a grin.

Catania looked down at herself and saw she was still wearing only the filthy rag that covered almost none of her burnt skin. "Have you got anything I can cover myself with?" she asked quietly.

"Certainly, Ma'am," the young boy answered quickly. He disappeared for a second and returned with some cloth no bigger than the rag Catania was already wearing. None of the men seemed to realise.

"Erm, thank you," Catania said as she took the cloth, and the boy beamed with delight.

"Yer look a tad thirsty, Ma'am. Can we ge' yer a drink?" another of the men asked. He was old enough to be the boy's father. He had greying hair and deep lines around his eyes, but the same unusual accent.

"Please," Catania answered, wondering why he'd needed to ask.

"An' yer look 'ungry too, Ma'am. Would yer like some grub?"

"Grub?" she asked.

"Yeah, yer know… food!"

"Oh. Yes, please."

Catania was handed a flask of water and some staling bread. The water was warm but refreshing, and she was so hungry she devoured the bread in seconds.

"Tha' were very lady-like, Ma'am," the young boy said, and one of the men elbowed him in the ribs.

"Is Alticon okay?" Catania asked as she returned the flask of water to the men.

"Oh, 'e's fine, Ma'am. Jus' a few scratches. 'e'll be runnin' abou' again in no time."

Catania felt some of her worry ease, but she couldn't help thinking Alticon had suffered more than just a few scratches.

"So, 'ow much further is it, Pa?" the young boy asked as the men repositioned themselves and lifted Catania and Alticon again. "We've bin walkin' fer ages."

"Looks closer than it is, son," a tall, bald man replied. "We 'ave a few hours ter go yet."

"Oh, man!" the boy whined. "But me arms 'urt an' we've on'y jus' picked her-" he caught himself, "-we've on'y jus' picked *Ma'am* up again."

The men started walking and Catania looked in the direction they were headed. She could see the huge defensive wall of Tallarin on the horizon, and on either side of it, the mountains stood high and mighty. The freckly boy was right, the city did look closer than a few hours away. But the vast area of sand between themselves and their destination was obviously distorting their perspective.

"What are you all doing out here?" Catania asked. "You're a long way from safety."

"Oh, jus' a bit o' this an' a bit o' tha'," a fat, red-faced man replied. "Nothin' essential."

"Well, I'm glad you found us."

"The pleasure is all ours," he replied.

The men bowed, and Catania closed her sleepy eyes. For a while, there was only the sound of feet scuffing sand, but then the men fell into conversation.

The heat of the sun above and the soft rocking of the board beneath Catania were relaxing, and she started to drift as she listened to the voices around her.

"She migh' do the cookin' an' cleanin', but wha' else does she do?" one was saying rather unhappily. "I travel fer days at a time an' when I return, she talks abou' 'ow difficult it's bin ter do the gardenin'!"

The other men started to laugh. "She's got yer where she wants yer, Polwit. Yer need ter show 'er oo's boss!"

"Show 'er oo's boss?" Polwit replied. "She'd beat me inter nex' week!"

The young boy was the next to speak. "I wish I 'ad a wife

ter do the cookin' an' cleanin'," he said.

"Yer mother does yer cookin' an' cleanin'!" his father argued. "Wha' d'yer need a wife fer?"

"Yeah, yer dun' wan' a wife," Polwit said. "They take all yer money."

"Bu' I ain't got any money fer a wife ter take," the young boy claimed.

Another man in the group butted in, "Hey, I 'eard Delwod won a load o' money gamblin' at the alehouse but din' tell 'is wife. When she found out, she took every penny from 'im and kicked 'im ou' the 'ouse. Poor man's lost 'is 'ome an' ain't got two coins o' winnin's ter rub ter'gether!"

"These women are all the same!" a new voice grumbled. "We should gather up all the men in Tallarin an' do summin' abou' it!"

"Women aren't ter be messed with. Ter do so would be at yer own peril. Sometimes it's jus' best ter leave 'em be."

Catania smiled to herself for the first time in a long while. These men were so strange and spoke in such an odd way she couldn't help but feel happier. Soon, she could no longer feel her pain, and she had completely forgotten that her father was inside her head. In the company of these bizarre men, her life was okay, and she could sleep without the disturbance of dreams.

THIRTEEN

Sparring With A Female

Oracus awoke to the sound of birds singing outside his window. It was early morning and a slither of sunlight was creeping through the window into his palace room. He had dreamt about Catania again, and now he was certain his dreams were actually visions. Catania *was* the Princess of Tallarin, the same woman who had been discussed during the meeting in the council room. He had seen her crossing endless desert with her Wolf, Alticon. They had been set free by the King and were returning to Tallarin.

Oracus sat up in his bed and looked at Bandor. Together, they had been in Afarra for several weeks now, and the Lavorian had grown to an impressive size already. When he stood up, he was as tall as Oracus's chest, and his mane was developing and beginning to shroud his face. But right now, he was curled into a small ball in the corner of the room, deep in sleep and completely peaceful.

Oracus and Bandor had been training their connection regularly and constantly speaking to each other through their minds since their arrival in Afarra. Through dedication and lots of practise, it became easier for them both to access each other's minds, and now Oracus could connect with Bandor without losing focus on his surroundings.

Oracus had also been sparring regularly with Garrin. At dawn almost every morning, they would meet in the sparring area and swing their swords at one another. For the most part, Garrin would be victorious, but occasionally Oracus would deal him a painful blow and put him on the floor.

But despite the successes in most aspects of his training, Oracus had managed no further development of his power. In fact, since throwing the goblet across the council room with his mind, he hadn't been able to access his power again, not even once. But it wasn't for the want of trying. He had attempted to move goblets at every meal-time since, and he had even sat in the airless council room until the heat began to send him to sleep, in the hope that it would awaken his power again. But so far, he'd had no luck, and it made him ever more frustrated.

In the corner of the room, Bandor fidgeted, and Oracus's thoughts returned to his dream about Catania. He'd discussed his previous dreams with his Lavorian quite regularly, so he was eager to share the latest one too. He focused on the Lion's mind and connected.

"Wakey, wakey!" he said.

Bandor's body remained still, but his mind stirred. *"Morning,"* he replied.

"I've had another dream."

"About Catania?" Bandor assumed.

"Yes, the Princess of Tallarin…"

Bandor lifted his head and turned to Oracus. "She is the

Princess?" he said out loud.

"She was travelling to Tallarin with Alticon," Oracus answered, returning the conversation to their minds. *"The King is in control of her somehow, and he's sent her to Tallarin so he can rule the city through her."*

Bandor thought for a moment, *"And this dream felt as real as the others?"*

"Even more real," Oracus said with a nod of his head.

"Then I think you should speak to Torvanon."

Oracus sighed, *"I don't want to, Bandor. Whoever I tell will think I'm crazy – even Torvanon. The people here have been good to me. I don't want to ruin my relationships with them because I have strange dreams."*

Bandor didn't reply but Oracus could sense he disagreed.

"I think the only way we can understand this is if we travel to Tallarin," Oracus claimed.

"You want us to travel there?" Bandor questioned. *"We don't even know where it is."*

"I know we don't, but I'm sure we'll find some answers there."

"We've only been in Afarra a few weeks. Are you sure you're ready to leave already?"

"No, but we'll have to see other parts of Pharia soon anyway if this war is building like everyone says it is. At least leaving would be our decision this time and not somebody else's."

"But if the King is controlling Catania, won't we be in danger there?"

"If these dreams are real, Bandor, then Catania thinks she has to deal with this alone. But we can help her!"

"And how do you expect to help her if the King is controlling her?"

"I don't know. But we've got to try."

"And if it turns out the dreams are only dreams," Bandor said. *"What then?"*

"I really don't think they are," Oracus answered. *"I'm convinced I'm seeing her for a reason."*

Bandor stood and padded across the room to the side of Oracus's bed. Oracus could tell he was against the idea. He thought it would be smarter and safer to remain in Afarra where huge walls and other Riders could help protect them.

"I can see this is important to you," Bandor said anyway. *"I don't think it's the wisest choice, but if your decision is to travel to Tallarin, then I'll stand by you the whole way."*

Oracus smiled warmly and patted the Lion's head. "Thank you," he said out loud.

*

It was the time of year when temperatures began to dwindle. Autumn clouds were covering the summer sun and the trees were shedding their browning leaves. There were cool breezes in Afarra, and sword training was finally becoming more bearable.

Oracus was wearing his green leather for another morning with Garrin. The sparring area was empty again, as it always was at this hour, and Oracus and Garrin stood alone. But when they had donned their helmets and were preparing to fight, a shout came from the palace doors and both Oracus and Garrin turned to look.

Kivali marched purposefully across the gravel towards them. She wore polished leather armour from her shoulders to her legs, all with a tinge of blue, and she held a sword in one hand and a wooden shield in the other. Her dark brown hair was tied back, and her blue eyes sparkled.

"Is everything okay?" Garrin asked her.

"I've come to spar with Oracus," she answered.

"We were just about to start actually," Garrin said.

"Then I'm just in time."

"But we're trying to stick to a schedule here!"

"It'll do him good to train with someone other than you, Garrin," Kivali claimed. She smiled at Oracus. "I'm sure he doesn't mind."

Oracus shook his head. "I guess not."

"I'll leave you to it then," Garrin said with a shrug. "I'll get some breakfast and relax instead."

He strode away and left Oracus and Kivali alone. Oracus looked at her and felt a warmth in his cheeks. He hadn't spoken to Kivali much before, but she had caught him staring at her once or twice during evening feasts.

"Have you fought a woman before?" she asked.

"Women didn't learn to fight with swords in the village I'm from," Oracus replied. "So you're the first."

"There's no need to take it easy on me," she said. "I can more than hold my own."

Oracus couldn't help but size her up. Kivali wasn't short, but neither was she tall nor powerfully built. And in no way did she look fierce, so it worried him that he might hurt her if he struck her too hard with his sword.

"Are you ready?" she prompted.

Oracus nodded and raised his weapon. He had no shield to protect himself, so had to rely on his blade, whereas Kivali was already crouched behind her shield and peering at Oracus over the top of it.

Since starting his training with Garrin, Oracus had learned to be more patient. He often waited for his opponent to strike first now, instead of committing himself and getting hurt. And as Kivali began to circle him, he decided that allowing her to make the first move would be to his advantage. But when Kivali did strike, her movement was so fast and aggressive that Oracus barely blocked it, and he staggered backwards in surprise. Any doubts Oracus had about Kivali's fierceness were quickly erased when she swung for his head, kicked him in the chest, swiped his legs from beneath him, and knelt on his chest in victory.

"You underestimated me," Kivali said calmly.

"Yeah, I think I did," Oracus grunted.

Kivali released him and offered a hand to help him up. "I did warn you."

Oracus brushed the dust off himself. "I just wasn't expecting *that*."

"Well now you know," she said. "Ready for round two?"

"Definitely," Oracus replied.

A similar ending followed round two. And for the next hour, Oracus endured the same helpless feeling that had plagued him when first sparring with Garrin. He got knocked down again and again, until his body ached, and his armour was filthy and scratched. Not once did he defeat Kivali, and by the end of their training, he was exhausted and she looked barely out of breath.

"How did you learn to fight so well?" Oracus asked as they sat down to rest beside the meadow.

"I've been using a sword since I was a small child," she said. "And there's a good trainer in Tallarin too."

"Are you going back there soon?"

"Quent and I have been planning the trip for a while now. We'll leave in a week."

A sudden idea came to Oracus and the words came tumbling out of his mouth before he could stop them, "Do you think Bandor and I would be allowed to travel with you?"

Kivali looked at him curiously. "You want to leave Afarra?" she said. "You only arrived here a few weeks ago, didn't you?"

"I just feel like I need to go to Tallarin," he said.

"Why?"

Oracus paused, unsure what to say without uncovering his dreams about Catania. "I think I need to learn more about Pharia before I'm ready for a war," he lied cleverly. "There's so much I don't know yet."

"Is it true that nobody from your village knew about Jowra or the uprising against him?"

"I don't know," Oracus answered honestly. "I think some people knew more than they claimed to know. Garrin, for example, or the old man who told stories in the local inn. And my father too actually, he told me he knew of Lavorians just before he–" A lump caught in Oracus's throat as he recalled the moment his father passed. He looked away from Kivali and fought back the tears. "How often do you travel here?"

"I'm sorry about what happened to your father?" Kivali said. Her hand gently touched Oracus's arm and he turned his head back towards her. "This is my first time in Afarra too."

"What did you come for?"

This time, Kivali looked away. "Just a change of scenery, I suppose. I miss home a lot now though."

Oracus felt her pain; he missed Thessley a lot too. He would give anything to spend a day there with everything back to how it used to be. He could sense that Kivali wished she was back home too, and together they let their minds wander in reminiscence.

"Shall we go and speak to Torvanon now?" Kivali asked after a moment. "I think we need to speak with him if you really want to join us on our journey."

Oracus offered Kivali a grateful smile. It was nice that she was so willing to help him.

"You should go and get Bandor too," she suggested. "I'm sure Torvanon will be more than agreeable if the three of us convince him together."

FOURTEEN

Preparation For A Dangerous Trip

It took a lot of persuasion for Torvanon to endorse Oracus and Bandor's departure from Afarra. Had Kivali not been there, he would probably have refused to let them leave. Torvanon was worried about their capture; the rebellion needed as many Riders as it could gain, losing one to Jowra before the war had properly started would be a huge blow, especially when he considered the journey *unnecessary*.

But with a well revised route of the trip from north-west to south-east planned with Torvanon himself, and Kivali's promise of keeping Oracus and Bandor away from danger, there was no reason for Torvanon to keep Oracus in Afarra against his will.

So, for the following week, Oracus prepared endlessly for the journey ahead. If he wasn't eating or sleeping, then he was training in the sparring area or visiting his father's grave or working on his connection with Bandor. Sometimes, he would sit in a quiet room and try to deduce his power. And very occasionally, he would take a lonely walk through the city and procrastinate.

When the day came for the trip to begin, Oracus walked to the field where the apple trees overlooked the ocean. He expected the journey across Pharia to be rigorous and trying, so he wanted to make the most of the peacefulness before he left.

It was a windy morning on the shore. The branches of the trees swayed clumsily, and the waves of the ocean crashed noisily onto the sand. Oracus's hair kept wafting across his face, and he repeatedly ran his fingers through it to calm it down. He stared out at the horizon while the crisp golden leaves rolled past him.

When the time came for Oracus to return to the palace and pack his supplies, he took a route through the city that passed the cemetery. He stood by his father's gravestone for a short time and let the tears fall, and then forced himself to go before he changed his mind about the journey. Oracus's biggest concern was leaving his father behind, but he assured himself the grave wouldn't disappear in his absence. When he returned, he would be able to visit his father again.

At the palace, Oracus changed his clothes and filled a pack with food and water. He attached a sheathed sword to his belt and hooked a bow and a quiver of arrows over his shoulder. Then together, he and Bandor navigated their way through the palace, and through the streets to the city gate.

Kivali and Quent were already waiting by the open portcullis when they arrived. With them, Garrin and Torvanon stood side by side, both smiling to hide their dismay.

"It's about time," Quent said with a sneer as Oracus and

Bandor approached.

Kivali was much less sharp, but she didn't look as relaxed as usual. "Do you have everything you need?" she asked.

"We're ready to go," Oracus answered with a nod.

"You can still change your mind though," Garrin said. "You don't really have to leave."

Oracus grasped his friend in a tight hug. "I need to do this," he whispered in his ear.

"You'll be back soon though, won't you?"

"As soon as I can," Oracus replied. "Maybe Jowra will be dead by then and we can return to Thessley."

"We can hope," Garrin replied.

When they let go of each other, Torvanon pushed Garrin aside and embraced Oracus himself. "Be safe out there," he warned. "And make sure you come back in one piece." He released Oracus but then held him by the shoulders at arm's length. He stared into Oracus's eyes and contemplated him. "It's been a pleasure having you here," he said finally.

Oracus smiled warmly, but Kivali pressed for them to leave and he turned towards the drawbridge. Looking back, he waved to Garrin and Torvanon. "See you both again soon," he said. And with Bandor beside him, he followed Kivali and Quent across the drawbridge and onto the vast fields beyond the moat.

FIFTEEN

Return To Thessley

The journey ahead was due to be treacherous. Oracus, Bandor, Kivali and Quent would travel through the Raspian Forest from west to east and only enter open land to evade Fervia, one of King Jowra's cities in north-east Pharia. They would then travel through the Eastern Mountains to Lalacia, another of Jowra's cities, to restock their supplies before continuing through the mountains to Tallarin.

Kivali and Quent expected the journey to span several days. It usually wouldn't take so long, but the direct routes and tracks through Pharia were extensively patrolled by Jowra's soldiers these days, and it was wise to stay well clear of soldiers, especially with a Lavorian present.

Since Oracus had been told the first part of their trip would be through the Raspian Forest, he had been thinking more and more about Thessley. He wondered if it would be possible to stop there on the way. But he was unsure about mentioning it to Kivali or Quent.

"Just ask them, Oracus," Bandor said. *"The worst they can say is no."*

"I guess so," he replied. He then disconnected from Bandor's mind and spoke aloud to Kivali and Quent. "Is there a chance we could go to Thessley?"

Quent and Kivali looked at each other. "Not a chance," Quent said simply.

"There are things in my house that are important to me and I didn't get chance to collect them before."

"Soldiers will be waiting for someone to return so we won't be going there," Quent declared.

"What if we–"

"No means no!" he snapped, and his big ears turned red with anger. "Get it into your head."

Bandor growled and Kivali looked from Oracus to Quent, and then back. "Maybe we could travel there to see if it's guarded," she suggested. "If it is then we'll travel around it, but if it's safe then Oracus can go to his house and gather what he needs."

"We'll be killed if we go there," Quent said sharply.

"Not if we're careful," Kivali assured.

Quent huffed petulantly. "Fine," he said. "But if we're caught by King Jowra's men then it's on your head."

It was still early morning and Afarra could be seen in the distance behind them. They were on the grassland that preceded the Raspian Forest, but the wall of trees ahead was getting ever larger.

"So how much further is it to Thessley?" Oracus asked as they approached the trees.

"It will take us until nightfall," Kivali answered.

"Do you know how to get there?"

"I think so," Kivali answered, nodding her head. "And Bandor should know the way too. Lavorians are pretty good with directions."

As they stepped into the forest, it seemed quieter than usual. Similar to how it had been on the eerie night when Bandor fell from the sky. Other than the twigs snapping under feet, it was silent, and thick shadows lingered in places they shouldn't. Somehow, Oracus could sense the forest was unhappy, and it seemed very unwelcoming, even to him. He wondered if the soldiers were still in there, cutting down its trees and lighting fires on its floor.

For several hours, the four of them walked through the undergrowth until they encountered the main river of the forest. Suddenly, from being surrounded by only dense trees and darkness for most of the journey, they entered a magical clearing where the autumn sunlight broke through the canopy and shined onto colourful flowers and the gently-flowing river below. There, the singing birds and chirping insects were in full voice, and their harmony mixed gloriously with the rippling water.

"This is the halfway point to Thessley," Kivali advised. She walked to the water's edge and refilled her flask. "Have a drink and take a rest."

Oracus knelt on the riverbank and filled his own flask; the cold water lapped pleasantly at his fingers and distracted him from the thoughts he'd been having of the King's soldiers. When his flask was full and he'd taken a sip, he sat down and propped himself against Bandor's side. He took in a few deep breaths and let the scent of damp wood and flowers linger in his nostrils. The smell reminded him of when he used to hunt. As he thought about the game he used to track, he unhooked his bow from his shoulder and flexed the string.

"I used to enjoy hunting here," Oracus said. *"It was always nice to escape the village."*

"Now being here scares you?" Bandor asked.

"It feels different," Oracus said. *"I just want to go back to Thessley and it be the same as it used to be."*

Oracus rested against Bandor again and drank some more water from his flask. He thought about Thessley for a while, and then watched Kivali as she kicked off her boots and dipped her feet in the water. With the sunlight shining down on her, her hair seemed to glow.

"She's beautiful," Bandor said discreetly to Oracus. *"You should go and talk to her."*

Across the clearing, Oracus noticed that Quent was watching Kivali too. He was sat by the stump of a dead tree and was craning his neck awkwardly to look at her. When he spotted Oracus observing him, he scowled unhappily and snapped his eyes away.

A moment later, Kivali got up from the riverbank and put her boots back on. She shook her hair and it glimmered some more, and then she walked over to Oracus and drew her sword. "Time for a bit of training?" she asked.

Oracus stood up and drew his own sword. "Sure," he said.

When they were facing each other in the centre of the clearing, Kivali began to swirl her sword through the air and tempt Oracus to attack. When he refused, she struck at him with as much speed and venom as she could muster. Oracus swiftly blocked the attack and the birds in the branches above scattered as their swords clanged loudly together. Kivali followed up with several strikes Oracus was able to parry, then she aimed stabs at his chest and he parried them too.

"She always leaves her right hip unprotected," Oracus heard Bandor say in his head.

Oracus continued to block Kivali's attacks until she left her right hip uncovered just like Bandor had observed. When the opportunity came, Oracus lunged and struck Kivali on her side, and then held his sword triumphantly at her throat.

Kivali winced and pushed Oracus away from her. With a groan of displeasure, she cursed him. "You were lucky," she claimed.

They continued to spar, but Oracus being victorious for the first time over Kivali seemed only to invigorate her. For the rest of their battles, she never exposed her hip again, and she continually dealt painful strikes to Oracus's arms, legs and body.

When they finished, Oracus washed his sweaty face in the river and splashed cool water on the worst of his cuts. By now, his one victory over Kivali was almost forgotten.

"Does Quent train with a sword?" he asked her as she joined him at the river.

Kivali raised her eyebrows at Oracus. "Does he look like he can fight?" she said quietly.

"Well, no," Oracus admitted. "But isn't it dangerous out here if you can't use a sword?"

Kivali laughed. "Quent considers himself more brains than brawn. He thinks he can talk himself out of trouble," she said. "Truth is, he's probably more likely to talk himself *into* trouble."

After resting a little longer, they progressed up-river until they found a narrow stretch of water where they could safely cross. Then, they pressed on through the forest until night approached and the light above the canopy started to fade.

"We should be there shortly," Kivali said as she ducked under a low hanging branch.

"It's about time," Oracus replied, yawning and wondering how much more walking his feet could take.

No more than a few minutes later, dim light trickled through the trees ahead and they emerged from the forest and onto the edge of a field that overlooked Thessley. To their right, Oracus spotted the old barn where he had first taken Bandor. And further down the field, his father's farmhouse stood abandoned and dark. Behind the village, the orange sun was beginning to disappear beyond the horizon.

"Come on, let's go!" Oracus shouted as the sight of his home filled him with excitement and longing.

Quent grabbed his arm with his long, bony fingers and hissed at him, "You can't just go stomping down there! Did I not warn you there might be soldiers here?"

Bandor growled fiercely and Quent quickly released Oracus.

"Go and get yourselves killed then," Quent spat. "Nobody cares if you die anyway."

"Quent!" Kivali admonished. "Will you please be civil for once?" She turned to Oracus. "He is right though. We need to scout the place for soldiers first."

Quent smirked over Kivali's shoulder before the four of them began to walk along the treeline. They moved slowly until they reached the bottom of the field, and each cast a sharp eye over Thessley for any movement. But by the time they came to the farmhouse, it was clear that the village wasn't being patrolled. By the look of it, Thessley had been empty for a long time.

Much to Quent's frustration, there was nothing to stop Oracus moving further into the village. And by the time they had stepped into the village centre, night had completely fallen. With the silver moonlight shining down, it was evident the King's soldiers had pillaged what they could from the stalls and shops before leaving. Oracus was saddened to see shattered glass and debris scattered over the ground. And he was distraught when they left the village centre and came to the wooden houses that were now no more than piles of ash.

Fearful his house had fallen to the same fate, Oracus quickened his pace through the village streets. Thankfully, the soldiers had left his home standing, and he sighed with relief. When he reached the front door, he paused and took a breath, wondering what horror he might find inside. But when he entered, everything was as it used to be, and his eyes filled with nostalgic tears. He was in the sitting room, where his father's rocking chair stood still and empty by the fireplace, and the scent of tobacco from his father's pipe still lingered in the air. There were work-boots on the hearth, with dry mud from the farm still clinging to them, and a deerhide coat hanging on a hook beside the door.

Oracus proceeded into his bedroom and found everything in there untouched too. His mirror hung whole on the wall above his desk, his books were still ordered nicely on their shelf, and his collection of swords were still propped against the foot of the bed.

Oracus grabbed the sword he had been gifted by his

father and studied it. It was sharper and cleaner than his other swords, and the emerald in the hilt was gleaming, even in the darkness of the house. He waved it in front of himself before fastening it to his belt, leaving his sword from Afarra in its place. Then he turned back towards the door and realised that Kivali was watching him from the doorway.

"Everything alright?" he said.

"Do you think it would be okay for us to stay here tonight?" she asked. "It's too dark outside to keep travelling and it saves us building shelter."

"I guess so," Oracus replied, unsure how he felt about staying in his home without his father.

"Good. I'll convince Quent we're safe while you start the fire and cook some food."

Soon after, Quent was sulking in the corner of the sitting area while the fireplace glowed orange and sausages from Kivali's pack sizzled over the flames. The smell of cooking meat had filled the small house and the warmth from the fire was making Oracus drowsy.

When the sausages were cooked, Oracus served them to Kivali and Quent, and kept one for himself.

"So, what's Tallarin like?" he asked Kivali as he took a bite. He was intrigued to know what was waiting for him and Bandor in the city.

"Well, it isn't anywhere near as beautiful as Afarra," Kivali answered. "There aren't any sandy beaches or courtyards full of flowers. There's just a lot of stone and dirt."

"It sounds like you don't like it," Oracus said, shocked by her response.

"It's not that I don't like it," she explained. "It's been built to protect the people from Jowra and his forces so there's nowhere I'd feel safer. But I would be lying if I said it was pretty."

Oracus took another bite of his sausage. "If Tallarin is so well defended, maybe Jowra won't bother attacking," he reasoned.

"Are you really that naïve?" Quent said slyly with a shake of his head. "Of course he's going to attack."

"It's more a case of *when*," Kivali added. "Tallarin is well fortified but Jowra is powerful and has other Riders fighting for him."

"Other Riders?" Oracus said, alarmed.

"There are a few," Kivali replied. "They protect some of his cities around Pharia and carry out his commands."

"And he trusts them all?"

"Well, I believe he scares them into obeying him," Kivali answered. "And fear can be as powerful as trust."

"You think they're *that* frightened of him?"

"Frightened?" Quent said with a snort. "They're all terrified of him! And rightly so."

"He's been a Rider for far longer than they have," Kivali explained. "He's much stronger and he has more than just one power."

"More than one power?" Oracus repeated. "I didn't know a Rider could have more than one!"

"Well, his power allows him to inherit another power from any Rider he kills," Kivali said.

"Are you going to tell me he's killed Riders in the past?" Oracus quizzed worriedly.

Quent openly laughed this time. "More than you'd dare

to imagine," he said.

Oracus looked to Kivali to deny Quent's response, but she nodded firmly.

"It's Jowra himself that controls the number of Riders in Pharia," she explained. "He tracks the Orbulars, the rocks that the Lavorians are born from, and has them delivered to him in Melzor where they're introduced to slaves. Once a slave becomes a Rider, Jowra kills the slave and takes their power for himself."

Oracus gasped, "That's awful."

"That isn't all," Kivali continued, her expression sullen. "When a Rider is killed by another Rider, their Lavorian loses its armour and becomes vulnerable like any other wild animal. Every time Jowra killed a Rider in the past, he took the armour from their Lavorian and somehow used it to build another Lavorian of his own."

Oracus's mouth opened in horror. "He has two Lavorians?"

"Two Dragons called Wravias and Pseubas," Kivali answered.

"Dragons?" Oracus stammered. He tried to imagine what they would look like, and how big they might be. No wonder Jowra was feared.

Bandor raised his head at the mention of other Lavorians. "Has anyone ever made a Lavorian before?" he asked.

"Never," Kivali replied. "If he hadn't done it, I would tell you it's impossible."

"And has he bonded with it like his other Lavorian?"

"As far as we know, yes," Kivali said.

From the corner of the room, Quent yawned loudly. "I think we should all get some sleep now instead of talking about this nonsense."

"We do have another long day tomorrow," Kivali agreed. "Let's get some rest and continue this conversation in the morning."

Everybody prepared themselves to sleep in the sitting area by the warm fire. Before long, soft snores were rippling through the room, but Oracus stayed awake for a while longer, reminiscing about his life in Thessley, and thinking over his fondest memories. Leaning against Bandor's side in his old home gave him a strange feeling of both comfort and regret, and he wondered if he would ever spend another night there after this one.

When he finally convinced himself to close his eyes, Oracus took in deep breaths full of the scent of burning logs and let the slow rise and fall of Bandor's chest send him to sleep. There, he dreamt about Dragons and Riders.

*

Bandor awoke abruptly and lifted his head, his ears raised attentively. Something had roused him from his sleep, but whether it was a noise or merely his imagination he was not sure. The flames in the fireplace had burnt out and left the room in nothing but darkness, but Bandor could see as clearly as if it were daytime. The others were asleep, all peaceful and still. Kivali and Quent were lying on the other side of the room, while Oracus had slumped onto his side.

A sound outside made Bandor turn to the door. It was probably just a rat or a fox, but his thin, metal tail flicked anxiously nevertheless. For a few seconds, he waited in complete silence, wondering if the culprit had gone, but then the distressing sound of crunching gravel and hushed whispers grasped his ears.

"Yes, he said he'd seen light in the window," one voice muttered.

"But nobody's been here for months, who'd show up now?" another voice replied.

"I don't know but it's that house there."

"The one with the fence?"

"Yes."

Bandor stood quickly and Oracus's head clunked onto the wooden floor.

"What's wrong?" he grumbled.

"They know we're here, get up," Bandor said sharply.

"They know who's what?" Oracus replied sleepily.

"The King's soldiers. We hve to leave. Get up now!"

Oracus almost leaped out of his skin, "The King's wha-"

"Ssssh, they'll hear you!"

From across the room, Kivali stirred. "What's going on?" she mumbled.

"There are soldiers outside," Bandor whispered urgently to her. "We have to get out of here."

Kivali came to her senses much quicker than Oracus had. She shook Quent's leg to wake him and grabbed the sword that was still attached to her belt. She moved silently to the window at the front of the house and then immediately turned away from it. "Everybody move to the back of the house!" she demanded. "They're here."

Quent scurried to the backdoor and Bandor watched Oracus follow him. But before Bandor could join them, the backdoor was hit from the outside with such force that it came off its hinges and knocked Oracus and Quent off their feet.

As the door crashed to the floor, a huge man stepped into the house and looked down at the mess he had caused. He stood taller and wider than any man Bandor had seen before and his skin was a dull shade of grey. He held a huge hammer in his hand, and his colossal torso was covered by crimson armour. The man moved further into the room and the broken door crunched under his heavy boots. He paused over Oracus's recumbent body and Bandor growled fiercely, warning him not to advance any further. But the man just smiled, and that's when Bandor noticed his eyes were as yellow as lamplight.

For a second, Bandor held the intruder's eye, and then he prepared to attack. But before he could launch himself forwards, Kivali's hand grasped his mane and the house started to spin around them. The man with grey skin and yellow eyes disappeared, so too did Oracus and Quent, and a darkness like Bandor had never experienced momentarily washed over him. Next thing he knew, he was stood beside Kivali within a dense patch of trees in the Raspian Forest.

Bandor was unsure what had just happened, or how he and Kivali had been transported out of Thessley. But when he looked up at her, he saw only an expression of utter terror on her face.

SIXTEEN

Elnir's Confession

Garrin found himself thinking with prolonged concern about his friend. Oracus had only trained for a few weeks before leaving Afarra and Garrin was worried he wasn't ready for the dangers that awaited in Pharia. There was the Black Forest to the far south, the Grevlors and Lisors in the Eastern Mountains, several of the King's cities throughout the land which were full of soldiers, the Riders under the King's command, and of course, the King himself. Pharia was a perilous place these days, and with only Kivali and Quent accompanying Oracus and Bandor, Garrin was worried about their wellbeing.

Garrin shook himself out of his reverie and focused on the task at hand. He was sat in the council room with Torvanon and Horvos, along with Elnir, the white-haired storyteller from Thessley.

"I have never told a soul, but I think it is time I did," Elnir was saying, his eyes wide and his old hands shaking apprehensively. "You need to understand I am telling you this because I want to help."

Torvanon had his fingers interlaced under his bushy

orange beard. "Please tell us what you know," he said calmly.

"Well, I was born in Melzor, the King's city, and I lived there for many years," Elnir started. "When I was eighteen, I was offered a job as one of King Amarad's guards. At first, I guarded the city gates and patrolled Melzor's streets, but I soon earned my place as a sentinel in the palace corridors."

"I was also one of King Amarad's guards." Torvanon stated, looking curiously at Elnir. "But I don't remember you."

"Yet I remember *you,*" Elnir replied. "And that is because you look the same as you did sixty years ago. However, I am not a Rider, so time has aged me, and I have become old and withered."

"But I do not recognise your name either," Torvanon expressed.

"Ah, well," Elnir sighed. "That is because Elnir is not the name I used to own. I'm sure you would remember me if I mentioned the name Fluzal to you."

Torvanon's eyes widened in memory. "That name I do remember, yes."

"I changed my name so I could try and forget my dreadful past," Elnir explained. "When you left the city, Torvanon, most of the King's guards and soldiers left with you. But being young and foolish, I stayed for a part in Jowra's domination. For several years, Jowra travelled with Wravias and took control of cities and villages all over Pharia while I stayed and controlled the people of Melzor in his absence, feeding my hunger for power. During those years, Jowra became obsessed with Lavorians. If he wasn't brainwashing innocent villagers or building his army, he was researching Lavorians in old books and texts he had found in libraries throughout the land." Elnir rubbed his aged hands together slowly. "To my surprise, he returned from his travels one day and presented me with an Orbular. "A gift from your King" he told me, and it was the greatest moment of my life when that Orbular broke open. My Lavorian was a Boar; Suidae I called her. She was a beautiful creature and I loved her very much – more than anything I have loved before. And as a Rider, I gained the power of telepathy; I could read the minds of anyone around me. Jowra was thrilled when he found out, he was so pleased. But I stupidly misunderstood his pleasure. I thought he was happy with *me,* but it was my power that he cherished. Because of my power, he knew the thoughts of everyone we encountered, and those who secretly opposed his regime were killed for their treachery. I hate to think about it now, but I was the cause of so much death. And I was naïve to believe that my position beside Jowra would last forever." At this point, the old man's voice began to break, and he coughed before he continued. "The King's reliance on me was a heavy burden for him. I had a power he so desperately craved for himself, and he couldn't stop me from seeing his thoughts either. Incredibly, he didn't know what his own power was, even several years after becoming a Rider. No matter what he tried, he just couldn't discover it, and none of his texts or books gave him an answer. He became frustrated and helpless, and relied more and more on my power to maintain his reign." Elnir then rapped a knuckle on the table. "But in the end, his luck changed, and my world came crashing down at the same time. During an excursion to the mountains in the east, he encountered another Rider and killed him. Within a day, he returned to Melzor with a happiness in him I had never seen before. He had learned that by murdering other Riders, he would inherit their powers, and that meant there was no limit to how strong he could become."

"And that affected you because he no longer needed you or your power," Torvanon presumed.

"On the contrary, it affected me because he *did* need me and my power," Elnir answered. "I read his mind that day and discovered his plan to kill me and take my power. So I left Melzor with Suidae and travelled north towards the Raspian Forest. But Jowra and Wravias intercepted us before we could get there, and Suidae was killed by Wravias. She sacrificed her life to save mine, and I somehow reached the forest and found a tiny village called Thessley." Elnir nodded his head at Garrin. "Suidae was dead and I was no longer a Rider, and unfortunately for Jowra, my power died with her. I lived for fifty years in Thessley, and I regretted the choices I made every single day. If I had never become a guard in Melzor, or if I had just followed you when you fled, Torvanon, then I may have been happy in my old age with a family who love me and without the regret of a dead Lavorian." Elnir finished and swept the tears from his face with a handkerchief. He then pulled a smoking pipe out of his breast pocket and lit it.

"That's quite a story," Torvanon said. "But why tell us now?"

"I'm an old man with many secrets and not much longer to live. I needed to clear my conscience a little," Elnir explained. "And it was a way of warning you too."

"Warning me of what?" Torvanon questioned seriously.

"That Jowra will only strengthen as time continues to pass," Elnir said. "There's no time like the present."

"I'm not sure I understand what you mean," Torvanon replied.

"Jowra doesn't like risk," Elnir said, and he let a long stream of smoke flow out of his nostrils. "If he hasn't attempted to conquer this city already then he isn't totally ready. Why wait for him to be ready?"

Torvanon bowed his head. "Thank you for the advice, Elnir. You may leave now."

Elnir lifted himself gingerly out of his seat and returned Torvanon's bow. He then hobbled to the door and left a trail of smoke behind him. But before he left, he turned back and spoke softly, "Will anything come of me admitting my past to you?"

Torvanon paused for a moment before replying. "Losing your Lavorian is punishment enough. I won't be locking you away for something that happened decades ago."

The room fell silent as Elnir exited. Garrin and Horvos both looked at Torvanon for a clue as to what he was thinking, but the slight frown on his face gave little away.

Garrin always thought he, himself, had been carrying the biggest secret in Thessley since he had bonded with Aquila, but it had been nothing compared to Elnir's. And how wrong he had been when he had labelled Elnir an eccentric fool with a tall tale to tell. The man had once been a Rider, as well as Jowra's right-hand man.

"Do you really intend to let him live here without making him pay for what he did?" Horvos asked

Torvanon.

"You know better than that," Torvanon replied with a glance at his army's commander. "The man is old and full of remorse. It would be a waste of a cell if I ordered him to be imprisoned."

"Very well. But what if he speaks of his past to drunken men in the alehouses?" Horvos said. "It would probably get him killed and cause a lot of unrest amongst the people."

"As I understand it, he has told stories to drunken men for fifty years in Garrin's village and never once mentioned his prior involvement with Jowra." Torvanon looked at Garrin for clarification.

"I didn't know any of what he just told us," Garrin answered.

"Besides, the men in the alehouses here could probably do with hearing something entertaining for a change. Paying to hear a geriatric's outlandish tales instead of whispering about Jowra's oppressive tyranny will only do them good."

Horvos grunted in response and shrugged his broad shoulders.

"And Elnir does have a point too," Torvanon continued. "We've been waiting for Jowra to make the first move for years. And I'm beginning to believe we should be more daring with our strategies."

"You want to attack Jowra first?" Horvos questioned.

"It was what Garrin suggested in our last meeting, but I was quick to shoot it down to appease Quent and Kivali. I think I was wrong."

"Do you think we can succeed?" Horvos asked.

"I don't want to attack Melzor right away," Torvanon explained. "I want to destroy Alvoria first and get the soldiers home before Jowra has a chance to retaliate."

"But we don't know how well defended Alvoria is," Horvos claimed.

"That is why I want Garrin and Aquila to fly there first," Torvanon said. "They can scout the city before we commit to an attack."

Torvanon's sudden plan shocked Garrin and his heart began to beat faster in his chest. "When do you want me to go?" he enquired.

"Today," Torvanon said. "The sooner we start this, the better."

Garrin stood up and his body tingled with apprehension. "I'll be back as soon as I can then," he said. He then switched his attention to his Lavorian. *"Aquila, get yourself ready. We're travelling to Alvoria."*

SEVENTEEN

A Rider In Fervia

When he opened his eyes, Oracus's vision was blurred. At first, he thought he was in his quarters at Torvanon's palace. But he soon realised the bed he was lying on wasn't as comfortable, and the room not as bright.

He sat up slowly and rubbed his eyes. Then he looked around at what appeared to be a tiny prison cell. He was alone, and besides the bed, there was nothing in the room except a thick metal door and a small barred window. It was grey outside, and an unpleasant chill lingered in the damp stone walls.

For a short time, Oracus wondered how he had got there. The last thing he could recall was falling asleep by the fire in Thessley. Then he remembered Bandor waking him up. And then he remembered the door of his father's home being smashed off its hinges. Suddenly, a helplessness overcame him, and he realised there was a void in his mind where Bandor usually resided. For the first time in months, he was truly alone.

"Hello! Is somebody there?" he shouted. He got up from the bed and pushed hard against the door, but it didn't budge. "Where am I?"

There was no response from outside and Oracus banged his fists against the metal in frustration.

"Can somebody help me?" he tried. "I shouldn't be here!"

Still there was no answer, so he sat back down on the bed and pulled his knees under his chin like a young child.

For many hours, Oracus stayed on the bed and drifted in and out of sleep. By nightfall, his stomach was growling so loudly it was painful, and by the following morning, his head was hurting from worrying so much. He didn't know if he would ever be free again, and he had no way of finding out if Bandor was safe either. And what if Kivali and Quent were imprisoned too, or dead? Their fate would be down to him for suggesting they visit Thessley when it was entirely unnecessary.

From outside the cell, the sound of scuffing footsteps came. Then the heavy locks on the door began to clang and Oracus got fearfully to his feet. When the door swung open, he was faced with a creature that made him step back in disgust. It was as tall as a Human child, with no meat on its bones and long hands and feet. It had a crooked nose and two short fangs that crept over its bottom lip, and beady black eyes that narrowed under a savage scowl. The creature wore just a thin rag with string tied around its middle like a belt. And tucked inside the string was a sharp blade.

Oracus retreated some more as the creature approached him. It brought with it a terrible smell, and Oracus saw its pale skin was coated in filth, and there was an unnatural amount of dirt under its yellow fingernails.

"I hope you're enjoying your new home," the creature croaked. It placed a tray on the floor that carried a slice of mouldy bread and a bowl of lumpy grey soup. It then grabbed Oracus's arm and took a long, deep sniff. "Mmm, I love the smell of fresh meat!"

Oracus yanked his arm out the creature's hands and it cackled happily. It then hobbled from the room and locked the door behind it, leaving its awful scent lingering in its wake.

Oracus bent down and picked up the tray of food, but when he saw maggots crawling through the bread, he decided he'd prefer to starve than eat any. He took his place back on the bed and wondered why he had thought travelling to Tallarin would be a good idea. If only he had stayed in Afarra…

Another hour passed before the locks on the cell door were cranked open again. Oracus was expecting the same hideous creature to enter, but this time he was met by a man twice the size of any man he had seen before, with grey skin and cold yellow eyes, and a red cloak draped over his shoulders. Oracus gasped as the man stooped into the cell. He seemed to fill the room he was so broad and muscular, and there was a malevolence in his eyes that frightened Oracus.

"You are in Fervia now," the man said in a booming voice that shook the walls. "You are expected to kneel in my presence."

Oracus didn't respond, and nor did he kneel. He just backed up until he felt the cold stone behind him.

"I said kneel!"

The man took one step towards Oracus and struck him in

the face with a giant fist. Oracus felt like he'd been hit by a hammer, and he dropped to his knees. The man smiled sadistically, and a glint of pleasure flashed in his eye.

"I am Gravaz," the man said. "I am an Ulatori from the Black Forest, and I rule this city under the command of the mighty King Jowra's."

Oracus looked up at the Ulatori from his place on the floor. "Are you going to kill me?" he asked.

"That depends how open you are with me," Gravaz said. "Tell me why you were in the village where I found you."

Oracus touched his face where he had been struck and felt it beginning to swell. "I don't know," he muttered.

Gravaz raised his hand threateningly. "Do not lie to me!"

Oracus shirked away from the Ulatori. "I used to live there."

"Why did you go back?"

"I was travelling through the forest and decided to use my old home as a shelter for the night," Oracus answered.

"Where were you travelling from?" Gravaz pressed.

"I don't know," Oracus lied.

Gravaz's huge fist struck the other side of Oracus's face. He let out a yelp of pain and slumped to the floor.

"Where?" Gravaz demanded.

"Afarra," Oracus conceded.

"Where were you travelling to?"

"Tallarin."

"And who were you travelling with?"

"Nobody."

Gravaz's boot met with Oracus's stomach and he rolled feebly onto his side.

"One of your friends was captured too," Gravaz advised

knowingly. "Maybe I should torture him for the information instead of you?"

A rush of relief filled Oracus's body. If he had heard Gravaz correctly, only Quent had been captured in Thessley. Somehow, Bandor and Kivali had both escaped.

"Two others got out of that house before I could seize them." The look of disappointment on Gravaz's face was evident. "Who were they?"

"I have no idea," Oracus said, finding some courage now he knew Bandor was safe.

Gravaz sneered. He turned to the door of the cell and shouted through it, "Lapsin, come in here!"

There was a scraping of claws on the floor outside, and then a Lavorian walked into the room with fur armour like Bandor's. It was a Hyena, and it was as tall as Oracus, with a hunch in its back and froth foaming at its mouth.

"Yes, I am a Rider. And I know a Lavorian when I see one," Gravaz explained. "I saw a Lavorian in that house where I captured you. Now tell me where it is!"

Somehow, Oracus was able to keep his composure. "I'm not telling you anything," he refused.

"Then you will die here!" Gravaz bellowed in frustration. He swung his boot and connected fiercely with Oracus's head. The kick was so brutal that Oracus fell backwards onto the stone and tasted blood in his mouth. He groaned as the room began to spin around him, and he tried to sit back up. But Gravaz's foot came towards him once again, and with a strike that rattled his bones, he slumped sideways onto floor.

*

Bandor had been worried about Oracus for three full days. After the ambush on the house in Thessley, the King's soldiers had taken Oracus and Quent through the forest to Fervia. Bandor and Kivali had closely followed, but not once did they get an opportunity to rescue them. Mainly because the Ulatori Rider named Gravaz was always in close attendance. Apparently, Gravaz was the only Ulatori to have ever left the protection of the Black Forest in the south. According to Kivali, Gravaz had abandoned his people several years ago to fight for the mighty King Jowra – an act of betrayal like no other.

Having pursued the captors all the way to the gates of Fervia, Bandor and Kivali camped on the perimeter of the Raspian Forest where they could watch the city without being detected. Until dusk, they observed the soldiers that patrolled the outer wall, and they waited in hope that Gravaz would leave the city and grant them a chance to save Oracus and Quent. But darkness came without reward, and they both prepared themselves for a long, anxious night.

The crickets were in full voice beneath a crescent moon and a cloudless night's sky, and the creaking of branches above the forest floor made it feel like the trees were alive and talking to each other. Hours had passed since dusk, but Bandor and Kivali were still wide awake and watchful. For the hundredth time, a guard passed by their observation point with a fiery torch held above his head.

"I'm sorry I didn't tell you sooner that I'm a Rider," Kivali whispered once the guard was out of sight. "And I'm sorry I couldn't get Oracus out of there with us."

Since Oracus and Quent had been captured, Kivali hadn't said anything about how she had miraculously teleported herself and Bandor away from Thessley and out of Gravaz's clutches. But Bandor had soon deduced she was a Rider – there was no other explanation for it. In truth, he should have realised before then – the signs were obvious. She had skill with a sword even Garrin couldn't match, and she had been chosen by Princess Catania to deliver important information from Tallarin to Afarra that would have been invaluable to Jowra should he have intercepted it.

"My Lavorian's name is Onca," Kivali said with a smile. "She's a Jaguar."

"How have you coped with being away from her for so long?" Bandor asked.

Kivali's eyes filled with tears. "I haven't," she said. "I really miss her." She looked up at the moon and took a deep breath. "When I was back in Tallarin, some of Jowra's scouts had been spotted nearby and had fired arrows at the guards on the city wall. Onca and I, along with my brother and a few others, were sent to kill the scouts. We found their camp in the middle of the night, and we cut their throats while they slept. But we had overlooked their watchman during our attack, and as we left the camp, the watchman aimed an arrow at us. I can't remember if I heard the pluck of the bowstring or the whistle of the arrow as it travelled towards me, but it was then that I teleported for the first time and it saved my life. But the arrow that had been destined to kill me pierced my brother's heart instead." Kivali's voice broke but she coughed and steadied herself, and kept her eyes focused on the moon. "I travelled to Afarra because I needed to get away from being a Rider. So I left Onca in Tallarin to give myself time to think. I guess I blamed her for the death of my brother – if I hadn't bonded with her, then I would never have had my power, and it would have been me who died and not him. At first, it was a relief to not have her in my mind, but now I realise Onca is the one who means the most to me."

It had only been three days since Oracus's capture and Bandor was already finding it difficult to cope without him. He wondered how terrible he would feel if Oracus was gone for three months.

"When I was younger, I dreamt of living a different life and seeing what was beyond Tallarin's wall," Kivali continued. "Becoming a Rider has made my dream come true, but what's happening in Pharia is nothing like I imagined it would be."

"I don't think Oracus expected it to be anything like this either," Bandor said.

Kivali looked away from the sky and towards Bandor. She shuffled over to him and rested her head on his mane. "We'll get him out of there," she said. "I promise."

Bandor blinked and then looked up at the moon himself. He trusted Kivali, and he knew she would do everything in her power to save his Rider.

*

Icy water splashed over Oracus's face and he awoke with a gasp. Light was creeping into the damp cell through the tiny, barred window, and as Oracus wiped the water from his eyes, he was met by Gravaz's menacing frame.

"Get up," the Ulatori demanded loudly.

Oracus was quick to obey. He didn't much want to be beaten like the day before, and he stood up immediately.

"Follow me," Gravaz ordered. He stooped through the door and Oracus trailed closely behind.

Outside the cell was a short corridor of the same grey stone. One end of the corridor curved out of sight, but at the other end there was an unopen door. Waiting by the door were several other Human prisoners who all looked like they had been beaten as severely as Oracus.

As Oracus joined the queue of other prisoners, he noticed Quent was one of them, with two black eyes and marks all over his face. Oracus tried to catch his eye, but Quent didn't look up.

Gravaz led Oracus and the other prisoners through the door and down a spiralling stone staircase. At the bottom, they exited the building and walked out onto an area of dying grass. Beyond the grass, Fervia's buildings stood short but sturdy, and past them was the city wall and the tops of the Raspian Forest's trees. The sun was shining above, as it always did in the north, but there was still a gloominess to Fervia that made it feel unwelcoming. Maybe it was the dullness of the buildings, Oracus thought, or perhaps the layer of mist that lingered a foot above the ground.

It wasn't cold, but there was something in Fervia's air that made Oracus shiver. There was an uneasiness about the place. That was until he felt something wonderful fill his mind; Bandor.

"Bandor, can you hear me?" he whispered hopefully inside

his mind.

"Oracus?" came the immediate response. *"Yes, I can hear you! Are you okay?"*

"Better now I know you're nearby. Where are you?"

"We're on the edge of the forest and looking into the city," Bandor replied. *"Has Gravaz locked you away?"*

"I was in a cell but Gravaz has brought a group of us outside," Oracus explained. *"I don't know why we're out here. I think he's going to kill us."*

"Don't worry, we're going to get you out of there. Is Quent with you?"

"Yeah, he's here," Oracus said as Gravaz brought them all to a halt on the grass. *"Please be quick!"*

Oracus disengaged from Bandor's mind before Gravaz could notice he was focused on something else. The Ulatori's yellow eyes lingered on Oracus as the prisoners shuffled into a line, but then he turned to the others and addressed them all.

"King Jowra always offers a second chance to those who have been brainwashed by his enemies," he stated in his powerful voice. "If you pledge your allegiance to him, then your past indiscretions will be forgiven. And should you be worthy, you will join King Jowra's ranks. But if you are not worthy, or you refuse to be reformed, then you will be killed."

*

"He disconnected," Bandor said worriedly. "We need to help him."

"Where is he?" Kivali asked.

"He said he was outside with Quent. But he thinks Gravaz is going to kill them."

"Then we need to act fast," Kivali said. "We're going to have to teleport into the city."

"Right now?"

"If you want Oracus to live," Kivali answered. "But I can't get caught in a fight with Gravaz because I won't win. You'll have to rescue Oracus and Quent while I keep him occupied." She swung a leg over Bandor's back and straddled him. "Are you ready to do this?"

"Just one question..." Bandor said. "What's Gravaz's power?"

"Fireballs," Kivali answered simply.

The world began to spin in a mixture of colours. The yellow sun merged with the green trees of the forest, which in turn merged with the grey walls of Fervia. It was disorientating for a moment, but within a second, Bandor and Kivali were between two buildings inside the walls of the city.

Kivali dropped from Bandor's back and quietly led the way through the maze of grey stone. When they reached the part of the city where the buildings gave way to the vast area of dying grass, Kivali paused and peered over a short wall.

"I can see them," she said, turning back to Bandor. "But Gravaz is with them."

"What are we going to do?" Bandor asked. He could feel his heart hammering beneath his armour.

"I'll lead Gravaz away from Oracus and Quent," Kivali directed. "When he's out of sight, you get to them as fast as you can and bring them back here."

"And then what?" Bandor enquired.

"I'll try and teleport us all out of here," Kivali replied nervously. "But I've never teleported another Human before. I've only ever done it with you and Onca. I don't know if I'll be able to."

"There's only one way to find out."

"Then wish me luck," she said.

But before Bandor could, Kivali had vanished.

*

Gravaz kicked Oracus to the ground with a colossal boot. He was so powerful Oracus didn't stand a chance of defeating him. Especially given his lack of nourishment since being captured in Thessley.

The brown grass was brittle under Oracus's face as he lay and suffered the pain. He felt heavily bruised, and he could feel the warmth of blood on his tongue. Then the boot came several more times, each kick bringing him closer and closer to vomiting.

Midway through the beating, Oracus thought he heard a distant shout. Then the kicking stopped, and he raised his head hopefully. On the other side of the grass, a woman was sprinting from the outer wall towards the heart of the city.

A crazed bellow came from Gravaz as he was forced to postpone torturing his prisoners and chase after the woman. His huge feet thundered across the ground, and as he disappeared between the buildings, Oracus felt it was safe to push himself up onto his knees. He gasped a little and held his ribs, then Bandor's voice crept into his head.

"Get up!" the Lavorian demanded urgently.

From the opposite direction to where Gravaz had followed the woman, Bandor bounded towards Oracus with his silver mane reflecting the sunlight.

"You came!" Oracus said delightedly.

"Of course we did," Bandor replied. *"Now get on and see if you can get Quent onto my back too."*

Oracus ignored the pain in his body and mounted Bandor. Then he somehow managed to pull Quent up with him. *"How are we going to get out of here?"* he asked.

"I don't know," Bandor answered.

"What do you mean you don't know?"

"I left that part of the plan for Kivali to figure out," Bandor explained. *"Now hold on!"*

Bandor turned and ran back in the direction he had come from. Oracus managed to wrap an arm around Bandor's neck and hold Quent tightly too. To their left, a handful of soldiers had emerged from the buildings where Gravaz had pursued Kivali, and to their front, the outer wall of the city looked as solid as ever.

"Bandor, there's nowhere to go!" Oracus shouted in his mind.

"There's Kivali!" was Bandor's reply, his paws now pounding the ground beneath them.

Indeed, from the same buildings the soldiers had appeared, Kivali arrived onto the grass too, closely followed by Gravaz. Somehow, Kivali was dodging the balls of fire that Gravaz was conjuring in his hands and throwing at her. It was like she was vanishing and reappearing with every few strides that she made. In his state of terror, Oracus struggled to make sense of what he was seeing, and he wondered if Gravaz had dealt him one too many blows to the head.

When Kivali spotted them, time seemed to slow until it was almost at a halt. Several of Gravaz's fireballs exploded fiercely on the grass behind Kivali as she veered to her right, and then more fireballs narrowly missed her head. Gravaz was quickly gaining on her, but Kivali was now so close to Oracus and Bandor that Oracus could see the sheer panic in her expression.

Bandor and Kivali were running right at each other, and Oracus suddenly realised they were going to collide. There was no way either could stop in time. "Bandor, no!" he screamed helplessly.

"Don't let go!" Bandor roared in response.

As the Lavorian shouted, Kivali dived onto the ground and skidded underneath his stride. As she did, a huge fireball appeared from behind her and was heading straight for Oracus's face. With no time to react, Oracus shut his eyes tightly and braced himself for the intense pain that would follow.

But the pain never came. It was only when Bandor skidded to a halt that Oracus dared to open his eyes again. But now there was no fireball. And no Gravaz either. Somehow, they were all still alive and now outside Fervia's walls. Against all the odds, they had escaped.

EIGHTEEN

A Power Is Learned

The sand underfoot was as black as tar, and dark clouds were rolling in from the north. There was lightning crackling in the sky above and a thickness to the air Oracus didn't like.

"What happened back there?" Oracus asked Kivali as he jumped from Bandor's back. "How did you move like that?"

Kivali shook her head. "Not now. We aren't safe yet," she said. "We need to get into the mountains and hope Gravaz doesn't follow us."

"But you teleported," Oracus persisted. "Why do you have a power?"

Kivali ignored Oracus's question. Instead, she unfastened his sword from her belt and then lifted his bow and quiver of arrows from her shoulder. "I went back into Thessley after you were taken and I gathered these from your house. You'll need them if he comes after us."

Oracus took the weapons but more questions came to him and he failed to hold them back. "How did you both escape from Thessley?"

"Not now, Oracus!" Kivali insisted. "We really need to get away from here."

She started to run across the sand, and Oracus was forced to pursue her. Close behind them, Bandor followed with Quent still lying across his back.

The mountains seemed incredibly far away, and there was nothing on the landscape to hide them from Gravaz should he come after them. Oracus had been terrified when inside Fervia, but now he was free, the fear was doubled.

Maybe it was the fear that made him look back, or maybe it was the lightning that flashed directly above Fervia, but when Oracus turned, he saw what he had been dreading most. Gravaz was leaving the city through the gate, riding on the back of Lapsin, his Hyena Lavorian.

"They're coming!" he found himself shouting.

Oracus and Bandor began to run faster, but Kivali skidded to a halt. "Stop!" she yelled.

Reluctantly, Oracus obeyed, and so did Bandor. But Quent was less fond of waiting for Gravaz and he jumped from Bandor's back to continue his escape to the mountains.

Oracus pulled his sword free of its sheath and cursed when he saw how much Gravaz and Lapsin had already caught up with them. He looked at Kivali. "Why have we stopped?"

"We have to fight them," she replied. "There's no way we can outrun them."

Oracus knew she was right, but he couldn't help thinking standing their ground would cause them to be dead sooner. He shared the thought with Bandor, but the Lion seemed more confident now the challenge was closing in. *"We've got this,"* he said.

Oracus could now hear Lapsin's huge paws thundering across the ground, and he could see the froth spraying from the Hyena's mouth with every stride. His heart was thumping unpleasantly, and his sword was shaking in his hand.

But like Bandor, Kivali seemed to find a courage within herself that Oracus didn't have. "Don't let the fire touch you," she advised. Then she began to take steps towards Gravaz and Lapsin, faster and faster, until she was at a sprint. When her enemies were only metres away, she vanished, and then reappeared in just the right place to strike Lapsin's front legs with her sword. The blade didn't penetrate the Lavorian's tough armour, but it was enough to make his legs buckle and send him and Gravaz crashing to the ground. Lapsin's face churned up the black sand as he skidded to where Oracus and Bandor stood waiting, and Gravaz rolled across the ground until his huge body was face down and unmoving.

For a few seconds, nobody moved, and Oracus wondered if they had been victorious already. But then Lapsin raised his ugly head, and Gravaz started to push himself off the sand.

When Gravaz got to his feet, he was taller and broader than Oracus remembered. He was almost twice the height of a Human, and more than twice the width. And he had a hunger in his eyes Oracus didn't like. It was then that he unhooked a flail from his belt and let the metal spike dangle on its chain in front of Oracus's face.

"You almost got away," Gravaz said in his bellowing voice. "And now I'll have to kill you."

The Ulatori swung the flail above his head with one hand and magicked a fireball into the palm of the other. Oracus gulped fearfully.

"He's mine," Bandor said inside Oracus's mind.

The Lion ran and leaped at Gravaz, but the Ulatori struck him in the chest with the flail and Bandor landed heavily beside Lapsin. The Hyena was on his feet now, and he was stood over Bandor with his teeth bared.

"Kill the Lavorian!" Gravaz ordered.

Lapsin's jaws immediately clamped around Bandor's neck and Bandor kicked his legs helplessly to try and free himself. He whined in pain, and Oracus felt the Lion's fear inside his mind.

But the fear was quickly replaced by Oracus's own fury. He wasn't going to stand and watch while his Lavorian was killed. He was going to destroy both Gravaz and Lapsin, and there was nothing they could do to stop him.

There was a ruthless determination in Oracus he had never felt before. And at the same time, he could feel a presence in his mind he knew wasn't Bandor. Like in the council room in Afarra all those weeks ago, he could sense something else was in his head.

As Gravaz stepped towards Oracus, and as Lapsin's teeth sunk deeper into Bandor's neck, Oracus connected with the unknown force and suddenly felt his palms become extremely warm. When he looked down, he had a ball of flames clasped in his hands, and although he had never held fire before, he knew exactly what to do with it. With a cry of defiance, he lifted his arms above his head and threw the fireball at Gravaz's chest. There was a momentary look of shock on Gravaz's face, and then the explosion came, more powerful than Oracus had expected.

For a time, everything went black. There was a painful ringing in Oracus's ears, and he felt confused and disorientated. No longer was he angry, or thirsty for the death of his enemies. Now he was just hoping he could get up.

When he opened his eyes, he was looking up at the thunderclouds above. He was lying on his back, and his entire body was aching. It took a while for him to summon the energy to stand, but when he did, he was relieved to see Bandor and Kivali were already up and unharmed. Gravaz and Lapsin, on the other hand, were both unconscious, and Gravaz had horrific burns on his face and chest.

"Are they dead?" Oracus asked hopefully.

Kivali shook her head. "They're both still alive. So we need to get to the mountains before they wake up."

Oracus didn't need telling twice. He slid his sword back into its sheath and started walking towards the mountains. A hundred yards in front, Quent was crawling through the black sand, still desperate to get away from Gravaz, but his body not strong enough for him to stand. When Oracus reached him, he lifted him onto Bandor's back with Kivali's help, and then they all pressed on.

After what seemed like forever, and what involved a lot of looking back over their shoulders, Oracus, Bandor, Kivali and Quent finally reached the base of the mountains, where the black sand was replaced by refreshing greenery. When they found the path that would lead them south towards Tallarin, white cliff faces appeared on either side of them and made Oracus feel like there was nowhere to hide should he need to.

"What if Gravaz follows us here?" he asked worriedly. "We're trapped between these mountains."

"He won't follow us now," Kivali replied. "He'll need to go back to Fervia and take care of his wounds."

"How can you be so sure?"

"You took off half his face when you threw that fireball at him!" Kivali exclaimed. "He's in no fit state to chase us through here."

The concern of whether Gravaz was in pursuit or not began to fade, and with it, Oracus started to wonder how he had used his power again. This time, he hadn't just thrown a goblet across the sultry council room, he had saved the lives of his friends. But still he didn't understand *how* he had done it. And neither did he know what his power actually was. One time he had thrown a goblet, and now he had thrown a fireball. *What's the link between goblets and fireballs?* he asked himself.

For more than an hour, the group marched up the path through the mountains until the white cliffs fell behind them and were replaced by patches of small trees and bracken. They were so high now that fluffy grey clouds occasionally obscured the route ahead, and the temperature had dropped several degrees. Having been famished due to his imprisonment, Oracus had taken the earliest opportunity to devour berries from the brambles that grew beside the path, and he had stuffed his pockets with as much fruit as they would hold too. Following that, he had drank all the water from Kivali's canteen before they reached a stream where they could refill it.

"So how *did* you escape Thessley?" Oracus asked Kivali

for a second time since their escape from Fervia. The path their feet now followed was flat and winding, with thicket and boulders along its edges.

"I assume you've realised I'm a Rider?" Kivali prompted.

Oracus nodded his head. "The teleporting thing you do is quite impressive," he said.

"Thanks," Kivali replied. "It's the *teleporting thing* that got Bandor and I out your house."

Oracus bit his lip. "How do you make it work?" he asked. "Your power, I mean."

Kivali quickly interpreted the reason for Oracus's question. "Are you still struggling with yours?"

"I don't even know what it is," Oracus admitted.

Kivali smiled knowingly. "I'm sure you could figure it out if you thought about it."

"I have been thinking about it. But I don't know how throwing fireballs is related to throwing metal goblets."

"Were there people with you when you threw those things?" Kivali asked.

"You know people were with me, you were there both times!"

Kivali laughed and Oracus felt his cheeks flush. "Think about the people who were around you in the council room, and then tell me what happened."

"I threw a goblet that was on the table," Oracus said with a theatrical shrug.

"You threw a *metal* goblet when you were near Torvanon," Kivali reminded. "And then you threw a fireball when you were near Gravaz."

Suddenly, it clicked, and Oracus's mouth dropped open in realisation. "Are you saying I can copy the powers of other Riders?"

"Yes, I think so," Kivali said with a smirk.

Oracus looked at Bandor as felt his mind begin to spin. The Lion looked as surprised as he did.

"Does that mean I can teleport too?" Oracus asked, turning back to Kivali.

"You should try it," she urged.

"But I don't know how."

"All I do is focus on the place I want to go, and then…" she threw her arms up in the air. "… I'm there."

Oracus looked back at Bandor for some inspiration. *"Any ideas?"*

"You felt another presence in your mind when you used your power before, right? Why don't you search for another presence again?"

Excited, Oracus came to a halt and closed his eyes. He focused himself and felt Bandor's mind scratching against his own. But then he felt something extra; something unusual he hadn't noticed before. Oracus concentrated harder and managed to pinpoint the other presence, but as soon as he tried to delve into it, he lost contact and couldn't get it back.

"I almost had it!" he shouted as he snapped his eyes open. "It was right there and then it… wasn't!"

"Calm yourself," Bandor advised him. *"Maybe you need to be relaxed like when you were in the council room in Afarra."*

"Give it another try," Kivali suggested. "You shouldn't expect to do it on your first attempt."

"You're right," Oracus said. He took a deep breath and released his frustration. Then he closed his eyes again and tried to locate Kivali's mind beyond Bandor's.

It took a while, but finally the presence he had been searching for revealed itself. As his muscles relaxed more, the presence grew, and Oracus was able to connect.

With the connection came the tingling in his fingertips. He was close now, and he knew it. He could feel the world circling around him, and then he floated momentarily above the ground. But just as he was sure he was going to teleport for the first time, the connection to Kivali's power broke and Oracus was thrown painfully into the thicket at the side of the path.

From in the bushes, he could hear Kivali laughing. "You should have thought about where you wanted to teleport to," she said. "Maybe then you wouldn't have hurt yourself."

Oracus could only scowl as he returned to the path covered in leaves and dirt. And seeing that made Kivali laugh harder.

"Why can't you just teleport us all to Tallarin?" he said seriously. "I'm sick of walking now."

"Unfortunately, my power isn't strong enough to get us anywhere near Tallarin," Kivali replied. "Besides, I would have missed out on you making a fool of yourself if I'd teleported us there already."

After several more hours of journeying south through the mountains, it finally started to get dark. There were plenty of caves to choose from off the beaten path, and Kivali soon picked one that was large and safe enough for them all to shelter in. By the time night had totally fallen, they were eating over a crackling fire in the mouth of the cave, and Oracus was feeling emotional.

"Are you okay?" Kivali asked him, sensing something

was wrong.

"It's just being out here reminds me of when I used to hunt near Thessley," Oracus explained. "There's a freedom that comes with nature, and it's making me think about life before everything bad happened."

"You're missing your father?"

"Every day," Oracus said glumly. "But more so when it's peaceful like this. I just crave his company."

Oracus finished eating and left the others in the cave. He walked for a short while and found a ledge that faced west and looked out over the land below. In the silence, Oracus let a tear fall from his eye, then he looked up at the stars that painted a pattern across the sky. When he was a young boy, he used to lie in one of the fields in Thessley and pick out shapes from the stars with his father. They hadn't done it for so long. And now he would never get the opportunity again.

From behind him, he heard Bandor's solid paws on the rock. He wiped his face and offered a weak smile to his Lavorian. *"It's wonderful, isn't it?"* he said. *"I'd stand and watch this until I was old and grey if I could. When I see beauty like this, it makes me question all the terrible things that are happening."*

"It's because terrible people rule," Bandor replied. *"The beauty will be destroyed if we don't put a stop to it."*

"How do you know it isn't us who are destroying it?" Oracus asked sincerely.

"What do you mean?"

"Well, if Afarra and Tallarin joined Jowra and stopped the rebellion, would it bring an end to all the fighting and death?"

"Maybe it would."

"Then are we doing the right thing?"

"Yes," Bandor answered. *"Because we're fighting for the freedom that Jowra doesn't allow us. Without Afarra and Tallarin's rebellion, he'd control everyone."*

Oracus looked back up at the stars and wondered why he was suddenly questioning the war against Jowra. He was certainly against the King's reign, but he wasn't sure sacrificing thousands of soldiers to kill the King was a price that should be paid.

"Oracus, your father died under this man's reign," Bandor said. *"He wasn't killed because he was a threat, he was killed because he was free. Surely that's reason enough for you to believe what we're doing is right?"*

"I remember how perfect it was in Thessley. And being in these mountains is a reminder of that. We could forget about Jowra and the rebellion and live the rest of our lives here. We could enjoy every night under these stars if we decided not to fight."

"But you'd know that somewhere else in Pharia, another child's father was being murdered because of his freedom," Bandor protested. *"It's okay to be scared of the task, Oracus, but I think that fighting is the correct route to take."*

"I know it is," Oracus confessed. *"I just wish there was an easier way to do it. A safer way."*

"But we both know there isn't. Jowra has to die, and you and I can't be living in a cave in the mountains while that happens."

"Do you think we can do it?" Oracus asked. *"Can we kill him?"*

"I won't stop until your sword has removed his head from his shoulders," Bandor said with conviction.

"And if we can't kill him?"

"Then we will leave him injured enough for somebody else to

finish the job."

Oracus couldn't help but laugh at the severity of it all. Would he really be willing to give his life to ensure Pharia was ruled by someone other than Jowra? Being a Rider came with huge responsibilities he hadn't asked for. It had been no more than a few months since he had left Thessley and now his life seemed to revolve around the potential comeuppance of a King he'd never even seen or met.

Oracus wondered if it was all just a nightmare he was due to wake up from. Maybe he would soon open his eyes and morning would be dawning on a peaceful Thessley. Under a sky full of twinkling stars, he wished for it to happen, but there was no waking up from this. His father was truly dead, and Pharia would continue to be in turmoil until either the King or the rebellion lost.

NINETEEN

Lalacia

Although still warm, the following day was wet and miserable, with lightning and torrential downpours hampering their journey. Just moments after leaving the cave, Oracus's clothes were saturated and uncomfortable, and he was reminded of the rainy autumns in Thessley when he had helped his father on the muddy farm, herding the cattle into their shelters. He and his father would return home and empty the buckets from under the leaky thatching, before they huddled around the fire to get dry.

Oracus, Kivali and Quent descended the path of the mountains in the early morning and left Bandor behind. They were to be staying in Lalacia overnight, and while Oracus, Kivali and Quent could slip into the city without drawing any attention to themselves, a Lavorian would stick out like a sore thumb. And it was best left to the imagination how the King's soldiers would react to a rebel Rider and Lavorian arriving in their city unannounced.

When the three of them reached the base of the mountains, they proceeded across the sodden sand (which was now golden and no longer the black it had been outside Fervia) until they could see Lalacia on the horizon a few hours later.

From having seen nobody since leaving Gravaz and Lapsin unconscious a whole day ago, civilisation suddenly came out of nowhere as they approached Lalacia's gate. For a half-mile outside the city's walls, foreign tradesmen and tradeswomen had erected tents and stalls on every spare area of sand, and they hollered prices to the hundreds of passers-by who squeezed their way to and from Lalacia's gates.

To Oracus's surprise, the city gates were wide and inviting when they reached them. The rain was still hammering the sand, but droves of people entered and exited Lalacia as guards on the narrow watchtowers to either side of the gate scanned the chaos beneath them. Oracus dropped his gaze guiltily as he passed, but nobody stopped him or even looked at him, and the gates and guards were soon behind.

"Welcome to Lalacia," Kivali announced.

The intermingling sounds of many voices and heavy raindrops hitting waterproofs was all that Oracus could hear as he followed Kivali and Quent along a broad street lined with shops. Everything and anything Oracus could imagine was displayed in one window or another; be it sweet or savoury food, expensive or cheap jewellery, sharp or blunt weapons, a wide choice of herbal remedies, clothing from nightwear to thick metal armour, animals used as household pets or farmyard animals, a great variety of different books, as well as ales and beers and wines, amongst many other things. For their time on the street, Oracus wished his power was to have more than a single pair of eyes.

"It seems strange there are no guards here other than those at the gate," Oracus observed. He had expected Lalacia to be somewhat less open than it was, quite like Fervia had been.

"This is Pharia's trading city," Kivali answered. "You'll see very few guards here."

"But I thought Jowra liked to keep everything under strict control?"

"Jowra is less blinkered than you give him credit for," Kivali said. "He isn't always focused on violence and death. He's been King for so long because he's wise as well as powerful. He's very aware that a thousand guards and sealed gates would only intimidate traders. And that isn't smart business."

"That makes sense, I guess," Oracus admitted.

"And letting these people feel free means their allegiance stays with him," Kivali added. "There aren't many who would oppose his rule and still travel here to trade their wares. And those who do oppose him, like us, are at risk of being found out and killed. It's a clever and cunning way for him to weed out his enemies."

Oracus looked around suspiciously at those closest to him and then turned to Kivali. "We aren't likely to be found out and killed, are we?" he whispered.

Kivali winked. "Not if we're careful."

For half an hour, they bundled and pushed through the mania of keen and wet tradespeople, and still more stores revealed themselves in an endless fashion. The rain had finally stopped falling, but most shoppers were still more than damp, and a fair number of puddles waited patiently to fill the boots of the careless.

During their walk through the city, Quent had begun to find his voice after more than a day's peace. Not until he started speaking again did Oracus realise how much of a blessing his silence had been. It had only taken the 'rude' and 'unfriendly' folk of Lalacia who barged into him to prompt his chuntering to return, and Oracus quickly became envious of Bandor still being in the mountains.

Eventually, Kivali and Quent led Oracus away from the jostling crowds and into a narrow side-alley that was as filthy as it was wet. The smell of sewage caught Oracus by surprise and he gagged momentarily. There was litter everywhere in the alley, along with rats scurrying from drain to drain, and several strange homeless people creeping in the shadows.

"Don't talk to them, try not to make eye contact, and don't accept anything they offer you," Kivali warned.

The vagabonds seemed to glide out of the darkness as Oracus passed by, and he quickly discovered they smelled as revolting as the filth they lived in.

"Jar of slugs, my dear?" a creepy old lady with crooked, blackened teeth offered. "They're poisonous." She held up a container with white goo smeared on the inside of the glass.

"Maybe you'd prefer a pair of pig's eyes, freshly extracted?" a tall, rangy man suggested. He was holding the two squidgy eyes between the thumb and forefinger of each of his hands as he showed them to Oracus.

"The rotting flesh of an eel?" a different woman with a frightening scowl proposed.

"How about a rat as a pet?" A short, gaunt man pushed

the other three aside. "We have lots of those here." He pointed to the edges of the alley where the creatures moved quietly, and an awful smile appeared on his pale face. "You may have as many as you can carry!"

Oracus grimaced and shook his head, and then proceeded along the alley a little faster, keen to get away from the vagrants that hassled him.

"Well, here we are," Kivali said a moment later.

They all stopped at a red door of a stone building that was slightly set back from the other buildings that adjoined it. It was barely ten steps from the frightening alley-folk.

Kivali knocked on the red door, and Oracus checked over his shoulder to ensure they weren't being approached by more of the strange people behind them.

There was a short wait after the knock, and then a woman's shrill voice screeched from inside, "Who's there?"

"Kivali and Quent," Kivali replied.

The sound of several locks being unchained came before the door creaked ajar. Then, a single blue eye peered through the crack.

"Who's he?" the woman's voice snapped.

"Oracus. He's a friend."

The door swung open and the owner of the shrill voice and blue eye stood before them. She squinted suspiciously at first, and then a smile grew on her gentle face. "You weren't followed, were you? Would you all like a drink? I bet you're hungry, aren't you? Where have you come from? Has the journey been exhausting? Quick, quick, come inside!"

The woman spoke with such speed that Oracus could barely keep up. As he stepped through the doorway behind Kivali and Quent, he glanced at the woman and took in her bizarre appearance. She was old enough to be a great-grandmother, with hair as white as snow and deep lines snaking across her face. Her eyes were severely crossed behind thick spectacles; her left eye was looking at Oracus, but her right eye was looking at something across the room. When she smiled, she showed a lot of gums but only one tooth, and her tooth overlapped her bottom lip quite significantly. She was surprisingly tall and gangly for her age, and Oracus wondered whether their close resemblance meant her and Quent were related.

The woman slammed the door shut behind them and started to reapply all the locks. Oracus took a moment to scan the sitting room he found himself in. It was relatively small, but equally as cosy, with a rickety chair beside the fireplace and knitting needles placed on a cushion beside it. There were ornaments on every surface, all meticulously arranged without a speck of dust. And on all four walls, there were dozens of golden-framed pictures of frogs and hedgehogs.

"So, Oracus, are you a messenger like Kivali and Quent?" the old woman asked as the final lock clicked into place. "First trip, is it? I sure hope they're both looking after you. My name is Eistra, by the way." She offered Oracus a huge grin, and her tooth and gums became even more pronounced. "Where are you from? You look like you're from Tallarin."

"It's nice to meet you, Eistra," Oracus said with a nervous laugh. "I'm actually from a village called Thessley."

"Thessley?" Eistra responded with a perplexed frown.

"Never heard of it!"

"It's in the Raspian Forest to the north. I was evacuated from there a few months ago when Jowra's soldiers found us." Oracus had a brief feeling of grief as his father's face flashed in his memory.

"I'm usually so good at guessing where people are from," Eistra mumbled, somewhat disappointedly. Then her eyes sparkled as she looked at Oracus again. "But you are a messenger, aren't you?"

Not wanting to dishearten Eistra further, Oracus nodded. "I guess I am, yes."

The answer made her beam with delight. "You've found a good one here, Kivali," she said with a wink and a giggle. She lowered her voice, but not so much that Oracus couldn't hear. "He's smart, charming, and so handsome!"

Kivali pretended she hadn't heard and kicked off her boots, but her cheeks reddened slightly and Oracus felt a pang of excitement somewhere in his chest.

"He's not smart!" Quent exclaimed, his voice as sharp as it ever was. "He almost got us killed on the way here!"

"You're always whining, Quent. Pharia would be far too boring if there was no danger." Eistra waved a flippant hand and Quent looked like he'd been slapped in the face, much to Oracus's delight. "Now then, should I assume you're staying for the night? I've made some lovely cakes that you could sample. Made with my own blood, sweat and tears – not literally, of course! I should warn you that I only have two spare rooms so two of you will have to share. One of you could share with me but I snore quite loudly. I'm so loud, I even wake myself up sometimes! I probably wake the neighbours up too. Come to think of it, that might be why they don't like me. Nobody really likes me. I don't know why. Perhaps I talk a bit too much, but it's better to talk too much than too little, isn't it? I certainly prefer someone who can make conversation…"

Eistra barely took a breath between words from when they arrived in her home to the very late evening. Twice her face turned such a dark shade of purple Oracus thought she might pass out. But she never did. He had never known someone talk so much, but listening to her voice was a helpful distraction from how much he missed Bandor. The distance between him and his Lavorian was too great for them to connect, and Oracus had become accustomed – addicted, in fact – to having Bandor in his mind. He felt incredibly lonely, even after just a few hours.

It soon came time for Oracus to get some rest. Eistra's cakes had been quite magnificent (Oracus had a hard time deciding whether she was better at baking or talking) and with a full belly after such a long day of travelling, he was struggling to keep his eyes open.

He retired to one of Eistra's spare bedrooms by himself after Quent had argued neither he nor Kivali should have to endure an entire night with him. A bed with sheets and pillows was quite luxurious compared to the prison bed in Fervia and the cold stone floor of the cave in the mountains, and Oracus prepared himself for a well-deserved night of comfort. But as soon as he lay down, thoughts of King Jowra and the rebellion began to circle in his head, and he felt wide awake again. He tossed and turned for a while, and then sat up in defeat when Eistra's snoring erupted from the adjacent room.

A soft knock sounded on the door and Oracus was

surprised to see Kivali poke her head into the room.

"You're awake too, I see," she whispered.

She pushed the door open and proceeded to sit at the end of the bed. She was wearing baggy blue nightclothes, and her hair was loose and messy. Oracus pulled the sheets up to cover his bare chest.

"Are you okay?" he asked.

"I'm fine," she said. "I just wanted to speak to someone."

"Didn't you want to speak to Quent?"

"He's asleep. I hope you don't mind."

Oracus shook his head. "I'd quite like to chat. I feel empty without Bandor here."

"I know how you feel," Kivali replied. "It won't be long now before I get to see Onca."

Oracus admonished himself for being so thoughtless. "I'm sorry," he said. "You've spent far longer away from her than I have from Bandor."

"Don't be silly," Kivali assured. "It was my decision to travel to Afarra without her in the first place. It's my own fault."

"You must really miss her."

"I do," Kivali agreed.

Oracus felt awkward and looked around at insignificant things in the room, like the cobwebs in the corners and the hooks that held the flowery drapes over the windows. For a short time, they both sat in silence, and Oracus pulled the bedsheet even higher up towards his neck. He wondered if Kivali might go back to her room, but after a while she turned to him and smiled.

"Can I show you something?" she asked.

Oracus nodded uncertainly.

"You'll need to put on a shirt."

Oracus swung his legs off the bed and pulled a shirt over his head. Then Kivali held out a hand for him to take.

At first, he could only focus on how warm and soft Kivali's fingers were, but then the room started to spin around him, and he felt a familiar weightlessness in his body until he was no longer in Eistra's house.

Oracus and Kivali stood alone in a courtyard, under the pearlescent silver shine of a mushroom-shaped water fountain. Beneath the starry sky, water flowed from the mushroom's cap and splashed lightly into the shallow pool below, while insects sang merrily in the damp bushes a short distance away. At their sudden appearance, a thousand yellow fireflies burst into life and began dancing around them in the warm night air.

"Where are we?" Oracus asked as he looked around in amazement. He let out a laugh of delight. "It's incredible."

"We're still in Lalacia," Kivali answered. "I found this place when Quent and I stopped here on the way to Afarra."

"It's so peaceful," Oracus said, unable to take the smile off his face.

"You'd think more people would come here to enjoy it, wouldn't you?" Kivali said with a shake of her head. "There's so much hate in the world that sometimes we should remind ourselves beauty like this does actually exist."

Oracus was reminded of his conversation with Bandor the evening before; when he had wondered aloud if it was possible to avoid opposing Jowra.

"This is when you preach to me that we're fighting Jowra

to stop places like this being destroyed, isn't it?" he said.

Kivali turned to him and offered a serious gaze. "Not at all," she said to Oracus's surprise. "If there was a way not to fight him then I would be all for it. But we have reached a stage now where a compromise cannot be made."

"Don't you think so?"

"Unfortunately not. There are so many people caught up in this war now there is no turning back; too much water has passed under the bridge. No agreement will ever be enough, so it will continue until the day there is a victor and a loser."

Oracus sighed, and the fountain suddenly didn't seem so attractive. The silver glow seemed less bright, and the splashing water became more cacophonous than therapeutic.

"What was it like in Thessley before you were forced to leave?" Kivali asked him quietly.

Oracus closed his eyes and let the memories of his childhood home come flooding back. He could almost smell the freshly cut grass from the summer fields, and almost hear the voices of the stall-owners shouting across the village centre. "It was perfect," he answered.

"Tell me why," Kivali pressed.

Oracus opened his eyes again and saw the fireflies had all disappeared. And the bugs no longer chirped from the bushes. "It's simple really," he said. "Thessley wasn't at war and I wasn't part of a plot to kill the King."

"I can't imagine what that must feel like," Kivali said. "I've lived my whole life preparing for war."

"That can't have been fun," Oracus presumed.

"Actually, the challenge of killing Jowra has always

brought me a lot of comfort."

"I suppose we all find comfort in what we endure as children," Oracus said.

"Did you ever want to leave Thessley?" Kivali pressed.

Oracus took a moment to consider his answer. Secretly, he had always wanted to see more of Pharia than just Thessley, even as a child. But now he knew what the rest of Pharia was like, he wished to be back in his safe little village.

"I thought the grass may be greener on the other side," he admitted. "But it turns out I was wrong."

"And that's why you're liked by so many people in the rebellion. You've only just learned of this terrible war, yet you're still willing to fight alongside us all."

"Jowra's soldiers killed my father, that's the only reason I'm fighting. I'm not brave or courageous, I'm just the son of a farmer who has been left with nothing but the hope of revenge."

Kivali bowed her head in acknowledgment. "Although I don't agree with the circumstances, I'm glad you left Thessley," she said. "Otherwise we might never have met. And that would have been a shame."

Oracus looked up at the silver fountain again. Temporarily, it appeared to shine a little brighter.

"We should get back," Kivali said.

Oracus nodded, and Kivali wrapped her fingers around his. For a second, they stared warmly into each other's eyes, and then the spinning began.

In an instant, the fountain was gone, and so too was the gentle splash of its water hitting the pool. Oracus and Kivali were back in Eistra's home, and the old lady's snores were continuing to shake the walls.

TWENTY

King Xarmoud

The next morning, Oracus awoke with Kivali firmly in his mind. He got himself washed and dressed, then made for the sitting room to see if Kivali was already up. To his disappointment, he only found Eistra, and she was rocking in her chair, knitting what looked like a very long scarf.

"Good morning, handsome!" she said as Oracus walked in. "Did you sleep well? The bed wasn't too uncomfortable, was it? What would you like for breakfast? Ham? Eggs? Bread? Mushrooms? Or just some oats? Maybe a bit of everything? You don't have to eat but a good breakfast will keep you going all day so I think you should."

Oracus had almost forgotten how much Eistra liked to talk. "Morning," he yawned. "I'll just have some oats please."

Eistra was on her feet and in the kitchen before Oracus had finished speaking. "Kivali left early this morning," she shouted through to Oracus. "I don't know where she's gone, but she said she wouldn't be long. Quent is still in bed, the lazy so-and-so. I should wake him up!"

Eistra talked incessantly while Oracus ate his oats. By the

time his bowl was empty, he was beginning to develop a headache, so decided to leave the house for a stroll.

"Be careful out there!" Eistra warned him before he left. And he could feel her crossed eyes burning into his back as he passed the strange folk in the alley ("Toenail soup, sir?").

Oracus turned onto the street where the many shops had intrigued him the day before. The rain was no longer falling, and the day's air was clear and warm, and Oracus doubted he would spot Kivali given how dense the crowds of people were. So instead of searching for her, he decided to focus his attention on the shops.

Every five paces there was a different type of shop to observe. With so much footfall through Lalacia, it was near impossible to enter every door, but Oracus made full use of the displays in the windows of all the shops he missed out. There were shops full of clothes: from battle armour to nightwear, both in a variety of sizes and colours, as well as silk linens, clothes for workers, day clothes, evening wear, hats, shoes, socks, and even fingerless gloves. There was a large variety of food stores too: butchers with chopped meats, grocers with fruits and vegetables, bakers with breads and pastries, and a fishmonger's stall too. There were also weapon stalls, with every style and shape of blade imaginable, while alehouses and inns made up the majority of the rest.

Oracus advanced along the street with endless enthusiasm until the gates of the city came into view. It was a disappointing feeling knowing he would have the return to Eistra's house, but before he turned around, he spotted one last tiny store that was almost hidden from view behind an apothecary.

Oracus approached the store with renewed vigour and grinned when he saw the fading picture of an open book above the door; it was the library.

The door creaked as he pushed it open. And when he stepped inside, it took his eyes a moment to adjust to the darkness. But when they did, he saw books had been piled everywhere. The library was empty of people, but there was barely room to move between the bookshelves and the mountains of tomes on the floor. There were more piles on and under tables, and there was even a pile that had been stacked in front of the window, which went some way to explaining why the library was so dark. The door closed behind Oracus, and his first breath was full of warmth and dust.

"Hello, my dear." The kind whisper of an elderly lady with silver hair came from between the shelves. When Oracus smiled at her, she disappeared again into the ocean of texts.

Oracus started by walking between the shelves and scanning the titles of the books. Any that caught his attention he would pull free and have a quick read of their pages. With each book he opened, more dust would rise into the air and make him cough, and he would close them more delicately before putting them back.

After maybe an hour, the library had seen no other customers and the silver-haired lady appeared to have vanished. Oracus transferred his search to the books on the floor and started picking them up at random. There were all sorts of weird and wonderful titles: *'The Governance of Lalacia: Volume I'*, *'Killer Snails? Protect your Garden'* and

'Controlling your Pets: Cat Psychology'. It was only when he held *'The Mythical Lavorian'* that he suddenly had his interest piqued. When he opened it to its first page, it read:

The Lavorian myth is that of a creature with extraordinary powers. When introduced to its Rider, a Lavorian breaks from its Orbular and takes the form of whichever animal it desires most. Its natural armour is impenetrable, and it will never cease to grow.

As legend has it, the Lavorian race was defeated and destroyed in The Noble War several centuries ago…

"This must be old," Oracus uttered to himself. Then he closed the book and returned it to the pile on the floor.

'A Woman's Guide to Male Behaviour' was the next book Oracus found. Then *'The Dangerous Ocean'*, *'Different Trees and How to Grow Them'*, *'The Fine Art of Cookery: Lobsters, Crabs and Shellfish'* and *'Building Your Home From Start to Finish'*. But then he found a book called *'Visioning'* and snatched it up with intrigue. As the book fell open in his hand to reveal a paragraph of text, he recalled the dreams he'd had of Catania.

King Xarmoud

Visioning, as mentioned in previous chapters, is a very rare skill. Those who have the ability to 'vision' are able to see life through the eyes of another, be it of either their past or their present. The visions are usually of random events and without warning, often revealing themselves in the form of dreams.

There is one name from history that is more associated with Visioning than any other – King Xarmoud. Although many claim Visioning is impossible to control, there are records stating King Xarmoud had harnessed the skill over decades of practise. It is said King Xarmoud could summon the power whenever he desired…

A pain came to Oracus so suddenly that it made him gasp and drop the book. What had been a minor headache earlier in the day had become a searing migraine that forced him to his knees. He reached out for a shelf to steady himself but grasped only a handful of books, and he dragged them to the floor with him. The agony was like nothing he had ever felt, except maybe on the night when Bandor's orbular had fallen from the sky, and he could no longer hold back his screams of protest.

When the pain finally subsided, Oracus breathed deeply and prayed the feeling wouldn't return. He dragged himself shakily to his feet, but then noticed his clothes were wet, and the wind was swirling around him. When he looked around, he was no longer in a cramped library full of dust. Instead, he was in the middle of a battlefield, surrounded by bloodied bodies on the saturated, sandy ground. Thousands of Human men clambered over their fallen comrades to fight the foreign enemy that faced them. Tall and pale, with black armour that glistened in the rain, the enemy glided like black liquid across the ground to slaughter the lesser Humans in their path.

A ferocious storm hung overhead, and powerful winds drove sheets of rain across the battlefield. Lightning flickered within the charcoal clouds and the cries of dying soldiers were lost in the claps of thunder that followed. Beyond the enemy in black, a city stood in ruin.

At the very centre of the battle, King Xarmoud held his ground. Under the thunderclouds, his green eyes surveyed the chaos with little concern. He held his sword in his hands, a sword with an emerald in its hilt, and he stood between the legs of his mighty Lion Lavorian. However impressive the enemy were at fighting, King Xarmoud and his Lavorian were more so. But their foes didn't fall to sword or claws, they crumbled to dust every time their armour was pierced.

For a long time, the battle continued. The storm was relentless while countless Humans were slain and never-ending droves of enemies came forwards. It seemed it would go on forever until a beast stepped out of the storm with an unworldly shriek. Both friendly and unfriendly fighters came to a halt at the sight of the creature, and a flicker of panic crossed King Xarmoud's face. The beast was as black as the armour of the fighters around it, and it stood even taller than the Lavorian it opposed. Three narrow crimson eyes pierced the weather, and a tail covered with spines swayed aggressively at its rear. Atop the creature, a magnificent being sat graciously, as pale as those under his command, but with armour more impressive and a giant sword in his hands with a serrated blade on either end of the handle.

It seemed this was the moment King Xarmoud had been

waiting for, because he quickly mounted his Lavorian and held its reins in a firm grip. Without a moment's hesitation, they charged at their foe, trampling anyone who stood in their way. The enemy charged too, and time almost slowed to a stop before they collided in the centre of the battlefield.

The impact sent shockwaves through the air, and an explosion of blinding white light erupted from between the two creatures and their Riders. But when the light dimmed, the four were nowhere to be seen. And neither were the thousands of soldiers who had been there moments before. There was now nothing on the sandy ground except silence and a lingering white mist; not a dead body, not a sword, not even a drop of blood. Even the storm had surrendered to the eeriness of the mist – the mist that signified the end of the war.

"My dear, are you okay?" a concerned voice asked from above.

Oracus opened his groggy eyes and found the elderly librarian standing over him.

"You're awake! Thank goodness," she sighed. "Come on, let's get you up."

The lady grabbed Oracus's arm and helped him to his feet. His legs were shaky and the warmth of the library had brought beads of sweat to his forehead.

"Thank you, but I need some fresh air," Oracus said as he pulled himself free of the lady's grasp.

"Are you sure you're okay?" she said. But Oracus was already through the door and out onto the busy street.

The journey back to Eistra's was a direct one, and Oracus no longer had an interest in the shops to either side of him. The dream – if a dream is what it had been – took precedence over everything else. It had been so realistic, like those he'd had of Catania. Yet this dream had been of King Xarmoud. And bizarrely, King Xarmoud had looked very similar to himself; his stature, his face, his hair. And his sword too, it had been an exact copy of Oracus's, with the same emerald in the handle.

As Oracus pushed through the crowds, he thought about King Xarmoud's Lavorian too; a Lion the same as Bandor, but larger. Had the dream been a vision of what was to come? Had Oracus just seen himself in the future, going by the name *King Xarmoud* and sacrificing himself on the battlefield? It seemed so ludicrous, but most of his life seemed ludicrous these days.

When Oracus finally reached Eistra's house, he paid little heed to the beggars in the alleyway, and he ignored Eistra too as he rushed by her to find some privacy in his bedroom. Lying alone with his face in his hands, he revisited all his dreams in the hope they would explain themselves. But something told him they were a warning of some kind. He pulled his sword from under the bed and studied it intently, hoping it would prove to be different to King Xarmoud's somehow, but there was nothing obvious. And then the words of Elnir the storyteller swam through his head – *"No two Lavorians are the same"* – and he wondered how King Xarmoud and his Lavorian could have been anyone but himself and Bandor.

Oracus tried to take comfort in the thought that even if his dream had been a vision of the future, he wasn't going to die in pain or by Jowra's hand. But unfortunately, seeing his own death, no matter how quick and painless, gave him no comfort whatsoever, and he continued to search for answers that refused to reveal themselves.

TWENTY-ONE

Grevlors, Lisors And Prisoners

Later that afternoon, Oracus said goodbye to Eistra and left Lalacia with Kivali and Quent. All day, Oracus had been longing to see Bandor again, and just as they reached the base of the mountains, he felt his Lavorian's mind scratching against his.

"Hello, stranger," Oracus said excitedly.

"I thought you'd forgotten about me," Bandor replied, his words echoing in Oracus's head.

"Of course not," Oracus answered. *"We just left later than we'd intended."*

"Is everything okay?" Bandor asked. *"I can feel your anxiety."*

"I'm fine, I think," Oracus replied. *"There's something I'd like to discuss with you though."*

Within an hour, Bandor had rejoined the group and they were following a winding footpath that directed them south between the high peaks. Oracus immediately told Bandor of his dream in the library, and they then spent the rest of the day debating whether it was a real vision or not. Bandor had suggested speaking to Kivali, but Oracus wanted to keep it to himself, at least until he had met Catania in Tallarin and had the chance to compare her to the Catania in his dreams.

Between secret chats with Bandor, Oracus would spar with Kivali. Since his single victory in the Raspian Forest several days ago, he'd been unable to defeat her again, and he was being struck down with boring regularity.

"Come on, Oracus. I haven't needed to use my power once yet!" Kivali cried impatiently as the late afternoon sun was beginning to set.

Oracus hit the ground again, this time holding his knee. When he glanced back up at her, she urged him to attack, and he duly obliged. When he swung at her head, she ducked, and as he stabbed his blade at her ribs, she vanished from sight, only to reappear behind him and hold her sword at the back of his neck.

"Let us hope King Jowra falls onto your sword out of pity," Quent chuckled with delight.

They continued along the mountain path until the sun had fallen behind the peaks and darkness had settled around them. Oracus's legs were beginning to ache, and he longed for a place to camp, but then Bandor stopped in his tracks and ordered them all to be quiet.

"What's wrong?" Oracus asked him aloud.

"I can hear voices coming from the path ahead," Bandor replied quietly.

"Then we need to get out of sight!" Kivali hissed urgently. She ushered them all into the thicket beside the path and they lay very still in the bushes. "Don't make a sound," she ordered.

Oracus peered nervously through the leaves until a

strange group of creatures passed them by, most of them chattering in nasal tones. The dozen creatures that were talking were thin and pale, with filthy rags that covered their torsos. Their fingers were long and dexterous, and their faces sharp and cunning, with fangs creeping over their bottom lip. Oddly, Oracus recognised the creatures, because one had served him rotten food during his short imprisonment in Fervia. The memory of the creature sniffing his arm made his shudder. The other three beasts that walked with the spindly creatures, however, Oracus didn't recognise. They were all big and dumb, with darker skin and a huge oval head on top of a thick neck. Their arms were so long their fists almost dragged along the gravel path, and as their stumpy legs plodded forwards, their bare feet scuffed clumsily on the ground. They wore only brown leather shorts, leaving their hairy barrel chests exposed to the cool night air. While they walked, two of the beasts were scratching their heads stupidly, while the other was smelling his armpit.

"Look, they have prisoners!" Bandor observed.

Oracus had been so interested in the creatures he hadn't noticed the two shackled men in the centre of the group. They both looked exhausted, but were being prodded with a sharp stick to keep them moving forwards. Oracus's eyes widened, and he wondered what might happen to the men.

When the group finally passed by and were out of sight, Oracus sighed with relief. "That was a close one!" he said. "It's lucky we have Bandor here or we would have ended up like those two prisoners." He stood up and brushed himself down. "What were those things anyway?"

"Grevlors and Lisors," Kivali answered as she followed

Oracus out of the thicket. "Jowra's minions. They search the mountains for travellers and take them back to his cities to be imprisoned. The Grevlors are the sly, sinister ones, and the Lisors are basically their bodyguards. But the Lisors are as stupid as they come."

Back on the path, Oracus started heading south again. Until Kivali stopped him.

"Where are you going?" she asked.

Oracus stared blankly back at her. "To Tallarin – as we have been for the whole journey."

"You're just going to leave those two men to be taken?"

"What are we supposed to do?" Oracus argued.

"Save them!"

"Didn't you see the horde of Grevlors and Lisors that were surrounding them?" Oracus pointed out. "What do we do about them?"

"It was hardly a horde," Kivali said with a roll of her eyes. "And it's your choice whether we sneak by them while they're sleeping, or we fight them and kill them all."

"I can't say I prefer either of those options to be honest," Oracus answered stubbornly.

"You're a Rider, Oracus, and so am I," Kivali said. "It's our duty to help those men."

And so it was that Oracus and Kivali followed the Grevlors and Lisors until they set up their camp. Together with Bandor and Quent, they watched from a safe distance while the creatures started a fire in the face of a cave, and then ate a raw rabbit each; meat, fur, bones, and all. In the corner of the cave, the starving prisoners had been tied to the wall.

"They're horrid," Oracus muttered as he watched a Lisor

scratch its bum and then pick its nose with the same finger.

As the Grevlors and Lisors argued over their sleeping arrangements, one of the captives started whimpering and begging for his release. "Please can yer let me go?" he pleaded with a sniff. "I 'av children at 'ome."

"Go and shut him up, Garumph," a Grevlor snarled at a Lisor.

"Do it yourself!" Garumph droned slowly in return.

"If you don't, I'll tell Gravaz of your disobedience," the Grevlor threatened.

The mention of Gravaz's name was enough to convince Garumph, and the Lisor reluctantly stomped over to the mumbling man and hit him hard across the face.

Oracus and Kivali waited until the group had drifted to sleep before they began their rescue mission. Their plan was to sneak into the cave and untie the prisoners without waking their captors, and then leave without them ever knowing of their presence. They approached the cave on tiptoe, and Oracus was so scared he held his breath until they were inside. The cave was dark, but the embers of the fire provided them with just enough light to see. There was an awful smell to the cave too, and Oracus attributed it to the filthy creatures that occupied it.

When they reached the prisoners, Oracus was quick to work on the shackles that bound them. But when the prisoner who had been struck by the Lisor awoke to see them standing over him, he let out a shriek of panic.

Kivali hissed at him to be quiet, but the damage had already been done. All around them, the Grevlors and Lisors were beginning to stir. And when they opened their eyes, they were shocked to see Oracus and Kivali standing in their midst. There was a short moment when everyone stared at one another, and then the aggressive shouting began and the scraping of metal weapons on rock rang off the walls. Within seconds, Oracus and Kivali's exit had been blocked by Grevlors with sharp daggers and Lisors with heavy wooden clubs.

"Very foolish," said one of the Grevlors in a creepy tone. He moved closer to them. "If you drop your blades then we may let you live."

"If you drop *your* blades then we may let *you* live," Kivali responded bravely.

The Grevlor's sinister scowl eased, and its face lifted into an even more sinister smile. It cackled unpleasantly, and then the cave echoed with the laughter of every Grevlor.

"You will die in pain, Human," the Grevlor said fiercely. It lifted its weapon to attack, but before it could even take a swing, Kivali had teleported behind the Grevlor and cut off its head with her sword. The other Grevlors and Lisors looked at each other as their friend's head rolled across the cave floor, and then pandemonium erupted. The screams and curses that came from the creatures was like nothing Oracus had heard before, and he suddenly found himself raising his sword to deflect the strikes from their daggers.

None of the Grevlors seemed to know how to fight, but with so many of them in such a confined space, they were difficult to defend against, and Oracus had no choice but to thrust his sword through a couple of their chests. The bodies fell at his feet, and remorse briefly crossed his mind before more Grevlors attacked him.

It took only a few seconds before Bandor was in the cave too, and then the Grevlors fell at an alarming rate until only the three Lisors were left standing. The fighting ended abruptly, and Oracus, Bandor and Kivali stood side by side, facing the Lisors who were twice their size.

"You should leave now before we decide to kill you," Kivali urged.

The three Lisors glanced at each other, then at their fallen comrades, before dropping their clubs and fleeing down the mountain path.

Oracus felt pleasure in their victory, but he had received a painful cut on his arm, and he noticed Kivali had blood on her forehead too.

"Are you alright?" he asked her.

She wiped the blood away and nodded. "I'm fine. Go and see to the prisoners."

Oracus had almost forgotten what they entered the cave for in the first place. Behind them, the two prisoners were awake and watching them, and Oracus approached them to untie their bonds. The prisoner who had shouted out and alerted the Grevlors repeatedly muttered his apology from behind a swollen face, while the other wouldn't stop offering his thanks.

When the men were finally free of their shackles, Oracus led them out of the cave and towards where Kivali and Bandor were helping Quent out the bushes he was hiding in.

"Well that took you long enough!" he said with a frown. "At this rate, we'll never make it to Tallarin."

"The coward would have stayed in these bushes even if the Grevlors had killed us," Oracus said to Bandor, and Bandor privately agreed.

"You're going to Tallarin?" one of the prisoners asked

sheepishly. "We live there. Would you mind if we accompanied you?"

Quent gave them both a derisive look. "So long as you don't slow us down," he said.

Now up to six, the group continued their journey south in the dark. The two newcomers were offered food and water, and after they passed a mountain spring where everyone could bathe, they found a cave of their own to camp in for the remainder of the night.

It was to take another two days to reach Tallarin, and Oracus prayed they wouldn't bump into any more of King Jowra's servants.

TWENTY-TWO

The Princess Of Tallarin

The next two days went Grevlor- and Lisor-free. Only wild birds and the occasional rabbit crossed the group's path. The weather was pleasant for most of the journey, except when the intensity of the sun became too much at around midday. But at least there was no rain, and that allowed the fragrant scents of the mountain flowers to spread.

Oracus and Kivali sparred regularly during the remainder of their trip, much to the amusement of their new spectators. Morpac and Uswir, as the two men had introduced themselves, enjoyed applauding Kivali's frequent victories and grumbling whenever Oracus's sword found its mark. Perhaps they considered Kivali the more attractive fighter.

But all-in-all, Morpac and Uswir were good company. Despite their ordeal, they were very friendly and told some compelling stories. Morpac, the prisoner who had been struck by the Lisor, was tall and slender, and he had no hair on his head. Other than the bruising on his eye and the redness on his neck where the sun had burnt him, he was very pale. Uswir, on the other hand, was dark-skinned and short. He was more muscular than Morpac, and he had a lot of dark facial hair and very bushy eyebrows. Both men were metal workers, and spent a lot of their time forging weaponry, so Oracus was intrigued by their knowledge.

By the time they were almost at Tallarin, Oracus had improved his power too. If he concentrated hard enough, he was now capable of teleporting short distances successfully. But being able to teleport during combat like Kivali had in the cave required a whole lot more skill. Every time he focused on using Kivali's power while they sparred, he would forget to block her sword and end up receiving a fierce blow to the ribs.

When the group eventually began their descent of the mountain path, Oracus had his first view of Tallarin's huge defensive wall. Strategically built between the mountains on either side, the two-hundred foot wall was black and intimidating, and shielded the city behind it. Oracus had seen the wall once before during one of his dreams of Catania.

"It looks exactly as it did in my vision," he told Bandor nervously.

The closer they came to the wall, the more colossal it seemed to become. And by the time they were stood at its base, Oracus could no longer see the watchtowers that sat atop it. At different levels, archers peered at them through arrowslits in the blocks, and Oracus's stomach squirmed with fear.

"Halt!" a voice bellowed from an aperture in the wall ahead of them. "State your business here."

"Two of us are messengers returning home," Kivali

replied. "Two are rescued prisoners. And the other two are guests from Afarra – a Rider and Lavorian, no less."

"You will proceed one at a time," the voice returned. "And if you disobey my commands, you will be killed."

With the sound of a chain being released, a thick iron door in the wall began to open. Behind the door, a man wearing a blue robe was waiting with his fingers caressing the handle of his sheathed sword.

"It's much stricter here than it was when I arrived at Afarra," Oracus whispered out the corner of his mouth.

"Just answer their questions and you'll be fine," Kivali responded.

Individually, the six were ushered forwards and each taken into a separate inspection room within the wall. In Oracus's room, a woman was waiting for him.

"Sit down," she ordered him.

Oracus took to the only chair in the room, it was metal and cold.

"Where have you travelled from?" the woman asked sternly.

"From Afarra," Oracus replied.

"And you have always lived in Afarra?" the woman said quickly.

"No, I lived in a village called Thessley until quite recently."

"What was your reason for leaving?"

"King Jowra sent his soldiers to Thessley and we were evacuated."

"And why have you made the journey to Tallarin?"

"Because I want to help you defeat Jowra," Oracus claimed.

The woman studied him closely for a moment. "And you're a Rider," she asked.

"Yes."

The woman considered him with narrow eyes for almost a minute, and Oracus looked down at his hands to avoid her gaze. "Very well," she said at last. "Welcome to Tallarin."

The others, including Bandor, were waiting for Oracus when he passed into the city. Beyond the wall was an empty square that came before dozens of buildings that stood almost as high as the wall itself and blocked the rest of the city from view. Most surprisingly for Oracus though, was how dull the city appeared, and how it smelled so fiercely of sewage and waste. Whatever he'd been expecting of Tallarin seemed now to have been wildly optimistic.

"Do you feel like we should have stayed in Afarra?" Bandor joked.

Morpac and Uswir said their final thanks and goodbyes as Kivali and Quent escorted Oracus and Bandor away from the square and along streets that led uphill towards the south of the city. Unlike Afarra, Tallarin's streets were desolate. There were no markets or shops that Oracus could see, and nobody was shouting the prices of their wares, just as there was nobody walking the streets for the enjoyment of it. Oracus assumed it was because of the smell.

When they reached the far side of the city, Oracus was already feeling homesick. But when they arrived at their destination, he was glad to be met by something that helped him forget the city he had left behind. A magnificent palace stood before him, carved into the face of the mountain that protected Tallarin's rear. The palace was spectacular, and a dozen or so turrets and watchtowers hung impressively over its grand entrance.

Kivali and Quent were first to ascend the steep stone steps that preceded the palace, and Oracus and Bandor followed them cautiously. They were then shown through the palace doors, and Oracus's jaw almost hit the floor.

The square entrance room they had arrived in was so enormous it put the palace in Afarra to shame. It glimmered magically with colour from floor to ceiling on every wall, and Oracus felt like he had walked out of one world and into another. A dozen doorways filtered into other realms of the palace and four spiralling staircases ascended to the higher levels. In the centre of the room was a grand white-marble statue of a man Oracus did not recognise.

As Oracus was led across the hall, he noticed several short creatures with a blue tinge to their skin that were doing strange things.

"They're Sashtrams," Kivali said, spotting Oracus's interest in the creatures. "They work here."

One of the Sashtrams staggered in front of Oracus with a huge stack of books in its arms. It couldn't see where it was going and dropped all the books on the floor when it banged into the statue. Meanwhile, another Sashtram had tied a rope around the base of the statue and was attempting to drag it. When it realised the statue wouldn't budge, it grunted unhappily and sat on the floor to catch its breath.

Reluctantly, Oracus tore his vision away from the comical

Sashtrams and accompanied Kivali, Quent and Bandor through another set of doors. This time, they were faced with a giant workshop full of machines making all sorts of noises. The workshop was cut in half by a walkway that led to a door on the far side. On the right side of the workshop, thousands of weird and wonderful items were being crafted. On the left side, the finished items were being inspected and tested. Amongst all the machines, Oracus was pleased to see hundreds more Sashtrams.

"They are such odd creatures," Oracus said to Bandor as he watched a Sashtram hit himself on the toe with a hammer and then hop up and down, cursing obscenely.

Together, the four marched along the walkway and passed through the door Oracus had spotted before. They came to a small landing with several staircases leading to higher and lower floors.

"We're going up this one," Kivali stated as she stepped towards a staircase on their left. The staircase arced to the right and Oracus couldn't see where it ended.

Ten exhausting minutes later and they reached the summit. Oracus put his hands on his knees and inhaled a few deep breaths at the top, while Kivali and Quent looked as if they could do it all again. They were now on a landing with only one door and a lone sentinel guarding it.

At their arrival, the guard grinned. "Kivali!" he said. "You're home."

The two embraced and Oracus felt a pang of jealousy.

"It's been an interesting journey," Kivali said. "We stopped off at Fervia on the way, and we also found some prisoners in the mountains."

"Sounds eventful," the guard responded. "And who are

your friends?" The guard was eyeing Oracus and Bandor with interest.

"A new Rider and Lavorian from Afarra: Oracus and Bandor."

"It's a pleasure to meet you both," the guard said, stepping forwards and shaking Oracus's hand. "I'm Sav." Sav turned his attention back to Kivali, but kept an intrigued eye on Bandor. "And what of Afarra? Did Torvanon have anything to say about Jowra's scouts watching our city?"

Quent interrupted at those words. "We cannot discuss such confidential matters with you," he warned. "It is for Princess Catania's ears only."

"I'm sure Princess Catania will be eager to hear it from you, Quent," Sav said in a tone Oracus found oddly satisfying. "Please, go straight through," he finished, stepping aside and offering them a final smile.

As they advanced, the door slid to the side, as if by magic. Then they were in a room that was undoubtedly Princess Catania's quarters. It was immaculate inside, and very white too. White floor, white fur rug, white walls, white shelves, and white marble ornaments on the shelves. On the other side of the room, a huge window offered a captivating view of the ocean, and Oracus realised he was now on the other side of the mountain.

With their arrival in the white room came a roar that made the hairs on Oracus's arms stand up. From across the room, a Jaguar Lavorian that was larger than Bandor bounded at them, and Oracus was sure it was going to kill them all. He threw up his arms to defend himself, but the Lavorian leaped at Kivali instead and knocked her onto her back. Oracus froze in fear, and then realised Kivali was giggling and the Lavorian was licking her face with what must have been a very rough metal tongue.

When the Lavorian allowed Kivali to stand, Kivali turned to Oracus. "This is Onca," she said. "And I've already told her a bit about you."

"I didn't hear you say anything," Oracus replied.

"You weren't supposed to," Kivali answered, and she tapped her temple with a finger.

"She only said nice things," Onca added in a voice that was smooth and delicate, like that of a mature woman. Her golden eyes met Oracus's and they were as deep as oceans and warm as fire. "I hear your journey didn't go as planned."

Quent was quick to jump in again. "If we hadn't brought Oracus with us we'd have been fine, but he seems to attract trouble."

"Is that true?" a new voice asked from the rear of the room.

Everyone turned to where four people – three identical men and a woman – stood in the window. Beside them, there was a white wolf twice as large as Oracus thought a wolf should be.

The woman of the group stepped forwards. "Is it true you attract trouble?" she repeated. She was perhaps forty years of age, but very attractive, with blonde hair scrunched into a tight bun and blue eyes brighter than the ocean behind her. She wore a laced corset beneath a flowing turquoise gown, and a necklace of pearls hung around her neck. Other than her cleanliness and fine clothing, she looked exactly like the Catania in Oracus's dreams. "I'm not a fan of troublemakers," she went on. "But I could perhaps make an exception for a Rider and Lavorian who are willing to fight for me."

"We aren't troublemakers, Princess," Oracus said with a slight bow. "We've just been unfortunate."

"Well, bad fortune does find us all during times of war," Catania agreed. "What are your names?"

"Oracus and Bandor of Thessley, Princess. More recently of Afarra." Oracus bowed again, deeper this time.

Catania studied Oracus's face, and he could have sworn her eyes flashed red for a moment.

"I have not heard of Thessley," she said after a time.

"It's a small village in the Raspian Forest, Princess," Oracus replied. "We were forced to evacuate when the King's soldiers found us."

"And that's when you travelled to Afarra, I presume?" Catania probed.

"That's right," Oracus said. "And I met Kivali and Quent there."

"Did you and Bandor bond before or after you arrived in Afarra?"

"The attack on Thessley was the day after we'd bonded," Oracus answered. "I think the soldiers found the village because Bandor's orbular landed so close to it. They must have tracked it somehow."

Catania's eyes fixed on Oracus again, as if she was trying to read his thoughts. Another flicker of crimson danced through them, making Oracus feel very uneasy, but he held her gaze nevertheless. Catania then looked away and shook her head. "Stooge!" she shouted. "Get some drinks for our guests."

From outside the room, a Sashtram popped its head through the door and yelled, "Yes, your highness!" before disappearing for a second or two. Then it returned with its spectacles askew, and its stumpy legs rushing along beneath it while it carried a tray of glasses full of pink liquid. The Sashtram offered the glasses around, bowing decorously as it handed one to Catania, and also put a glass on the floor in front of Bandor and Onca.

Oracus was just taking a sip from his glass when Bandor looked down at his own. *"What am I meant to do with this?"* he asked. *"I don't have any thumbs!"*

Oracus choked, and pink liquid came out of his nose.

When the drinks were all served, Catania ushered Oracus to the back of the room where the three men and the wolf were still waiting. The three men, Oracus noticed, were identical. Other than the colour of the robes they were wearing, they all looked exactly the same: thin and tall, with age lines on their faces and a long, crooked nose each. They had silver hair, and all three had swept it over their heads to try and hide an obvious bald patch on top.

"Oracus, please meet the triplets: Farlog, Shio and Croij." Catania pointed at each of them as she said their names. Then her hand pointed to the wolf. "And Alticon, who was my Lavorian a very long time ago."

Oracus's eyes lingered on Alticon. The wolf was sat, but its head was still at the same height as his. Its ears were up and attentive, and its eyes like ice. *"His name is Alticon, just as I heard in my dreams,"* Oracus said to Bandor.

"It's good to meet you," the triplets said together as they were introduced. They even sounded identical.

"The triplets are my advisers," Catania explained.

"Farlog is more knowledgable than anyone else I know. If he doesn't know about it then I wouldn't consider it worth knowing." Farlog smiled and waved his hand dismissively. "Shio commands my army. He trains the soldiers for battle and knows everything about war. He's been especially busy lately, as I'm sure you can imagine." Catania allowed the compliment to settle before she continued. "And Croij is an *inventor,*" she said. "He spends most of his time in a laboratory creating strange things with the help of the Sashtrams." Croij grinned happily. "My role as leader is much easier with these three men at my side."

Oracus was pleased to see everyone in Tallarin appeared friendly. After walking through the streets to reach the palace, he thought he'd made a huge mistake coming here. But having finally met Catania and her accomplices, he was starting to feel more at ease.

"I apologise, Oracus, but we must move on from idle chit-chat and concentrate on more important matters." Catania looked at Kivali and Quent. "What was said in Afarra?"

"Torvanon agreed to remain defensive. After a lengthy discussion, he understood attacking Jowra would only succeed in provoking him," Kivali responded.

"How strong are the forces in Afarra?" Catania asked.

"Substantial," Quent replied. "But not enough to rival the King's army. I think Torvanon believes himself and Ursus powerful enough to concern the King, but I suspect they would fall a long way short."

Catania sighed. "I doubt a man as wise as Torvanon would be naïve enough to believe King Jowra can be defeated by a single man and his Lavorian."

"Has anything changed here?" Kivali asked. "Any increase in Jowra's scouts observing the city?"

"Nothing to note," Catania answered. "We have forged enough weapons for every man in Tallarin to fight should we need it though."

"Do you know how many soldiers Jowra has?" Oracus questioned.

"It would be a guess," Farlog said. "But we do know his forces far exceed our own. Our advantage is that Tallarin was built to withstand huge pressure. It would take an army of an immense size to effectively breach our wall."

"Unless Jowra was to join his army's attack," Shio reasoned. "Then he'd just fly over the wall with his two Dragons and set fire to us all."

"If he is *that* powerful then why doesn't he just destroy Tallarin and Afarra by himself and be done with it?" Oracus enquired.

"Nobody but Jowra knows the answer to that," Shio said. "But it certainly suits me if he prefers to stay in Melzor."

"Are there any others fighting against Jowra?" Oracus asked. "Besides Tallarin and Afarra, of course."

"No. Just two armies in opposite corners of the land."

"Is it possible then?" Oracus said glumly. "Can he be defeated?"

Croij shrugged. "We won't know until the time comes for us to try."

The response didn't fill Oracus with much optimism. He glanced around at the others for some hope but found nothing except expressions of defeat. "Is it really that bad?" he said.

"Come now, enough of this," Catania deflected. "You

must be tired after such a long journey, and that's hardly helpful during discussions about war. I'll get Stooge to show you to your room. Stooge!"

The Sashtram came sprinting into the room, his blue cheeks carrying a pink tinge. He bowed so deeply his pudgy nose nearly touched the floor. "Can I help you, ma'am?"

"Show our guests to their room. Make sure they're comfortable."

The Sashtram nodded nervously and grabbed Oracus's hand. "This way, sir. Follow me," he urged.

Oracus followed Stooge, and Bandor trotted close behind. At the sliding door, they turned back to the sound of Catania's voice.

"Welcome to Tallarin, both of you," she said. "It's a pleasure to have you here."

Twenty-Three

Alvoria

Alvoria was a city only a few miles south of the Raspian Forest, and within a stone's throw of the expanse of water known as Bulu Lake. It was so small, it appeared to be more a village than a city, and when Garrin scouted it with Aquila, it had been remarkably unsecure. He hadn't witnessed colossal walls and vast lines of defences, with turrets manned by hundreds of archers. Instead, he had seen a few wooden buildings built upon a deep mine full of explosives, with only a hundred soldiers stopping him from wreaking havoc.

It would have been easy for Garrin to fly back to Afarra and allow Torvanon to decide how they should proceed. After all, he had only been sent there to observe. However, Garrin was keen to prove himself to Torvanon, and by destroying Alvoria singlehandedly, he would undoubtedly do that.

At daybreak on the day following his and Aquila's arrival, a large cart was drawn towards Alvoria's gate by two horses. Using Aquila's incredible sight, Garrin could see the cargo was stored in barrels, and that's when he seized his opportunity.

"This is our chance," he said to Aquila. *"Let's go."*

In a smooth movement he had made a thousand times before, he grasped the reins around the Eagle's neck and swung a leg over her back. Then Aquila took off and the wind whipped Garrin's blonde hair back and forth across his face.

When they had ascended to several-hundred feet, Garrin's stomach lurched.

"You're nervous," Aquila pointed out.

"Not of being so high," Garrin explained. *"I just don't want to mess this up."*

Beneath them, the horse-drawn cart looked miniscule. It was like an ant approaching the entrance to an anthill.

"Now is our time," Aquila stated. *"Prepare your arrow."*

Garrin took both hands from Aquila's reins as she hovered carefully. He gripped her back tighter between his thighs and then pulled an arrow from his quiver. With a match, he lit the arrow, and then nocked it to his bow.

"Are you ready?" Aquila urged.

"I'm always ready," Garrin fired back.

Aquila tucked her wings into her sides and dived towards the city gate at speed. This time, flying was what caused Garrin's stomach to lurch.

As Aquila came to a hover again above the city wall, Garrin could hear the frightened shouts of the alerted guards. He drew on his bowstring and released the arrow at the cart.

His shot was true, and the fiery arrow pierced a barrel. Within a second, the cart exploded, and a ball of flames rose up into the sky. The heat from the explosion singed the hairs on Garrin's face, and Aquila retreated to a safer distance.

"That was close," Garrin said, rubbing his cheeks.

"But it worked," Aquila replied. *"Look!"*

Where the cart had been passing through the city gate, a huge hole had been made in the wall and a dozen buildings nearest the explosion had been destroyed. A fire raged, and it swept through the city hungrily.

Many of the guards had died to the explosion, but the rest were screaming orders to their comrades in the hope of finding some organisation. Garrin and Aquila descended into the city and found a spot free of fire and smoke, but it soon became clear the enemy soldiers sought that area too.

Garrin loosed several arrows as the enemy approached, he then alighted Aquila and drew his sword.

"Keep them worried about what flies above," Garrin ordered. *"I'll fight them off from down here."*

Aquila did as she was told and took off into the air once again. Meanwhile, Garrin began to cut down the foes who reached him first.

The smell of fire and smoke drifted on the air, and Alvoria was soon a scene of devastation. As bloodied men fell beneath Garrin's sword and Aquila's talons, it resembled more of a massacre than a battle. And whenever the enemy appeared to regroup and come forward as one, Garrin would use his power to create a whirlwind of dirt that engulfed them and broke their unity.

"I think they're almost defeated," Garrin said much sooner than he could ever have hoped. As he spoke, an arrow whistled past his face and disappeared into the smoke behind him. *"Kill the rest of their archers and we'll get out of*

here!"

But the words had barely left his mouth when the ground trembled beneath his feet.

He stopped in his tracks and turned towards where the entrance of the city had been obliterated. *"What was that?"* he said.

It took a moment, but Aquila's reply came clear and fearful, *"It's a Lavorian!"*

Garrin's body filled with dread. *"Please tell me it's a friendly Lavorian."*

"If enormous and angry means friendly, then yes, it's friendly," Aquila answered.

Rooted to the spot, Garrin stared to the south as every tremor that followed came more intense than the last. *"Are those its footsteps?"* he cried.

It suddenly became Garrin's greatest wish that the smoke would keep him hidden. But when the Lavorian reached the city, it smashed through what remained of the wall and seemed to buffet the smoke away with its enormous body.

The Lavorian was an Elephant, and it was truly colossal. Each of its legs was like a tree that had been growing for a thousand years, and its body and head were beyond comparison. Beneath its searching eyes, its trunk swung like a giant pendulum.

Craning his neck, Garrin could see up to a man who stood on the Elephant's head, and he was so high up he appeared no bigger than an insect. But in no time, the Rider had jumped from the Lavorian's head and slid down its trunk with impeccable balance, before landing delicately on the ground a few yards away from Garrin.

"What a strange circumstance we find ourselves in," the

man said. He was a little older than Garrin, perhaps mid-twenties, and he carried himself with a sickening arrogance. He had short black hair and olive skin, and thin white stripes had been painted beneath his eyes. "I'm Zarad. And he's Mammat," the man finished, pointing first at himself and then at his Lavorian.

Garrin was too shaken to respond to Zarad

"A man destroys a city alone but is then too frightened to speak when faced by a Rider and Lavorian," Zarad said with a malevolent grin. "Surely not?"

"I'm not scared of you!" Garrin shouted, finally finding his voice.

Zarad seemed amused. "You realise this is King Jowra's city, right?" he asked. "Why would you want to provoke him?"

"Keep him talking," Aquila said inside Garrin's mind. *"I'll get us out of here when he's distracted."*

"More silence?" Zarad went on. "You must be really terrified." The Rider took several steps towards Garrin, leaving only a small distance between them. "I suppose I should give you a choice: you can either surrender and agree to join King Jowra's forces, or I can kill you right here and end this madness." He looked around at the buildings that were still crackling with flames. "What will it be?"

"I would never fight for Jowra!" Garrin exclaimed.

"So be it."

Behind Zarad, Mammat reared onto his hind legs and produced a deafening sound through his trunk. When his front feet hit the ground again, the force of the quake knocked Garrin off his feet and onto his back.

"Any last words before you die?" Zarad asked, now with

triumph dancing in his eyes.

"Aquila! Now!" Garrin bellowed.

Zarad looked confused in the second before Garrin flung dirt in his face. And before the King's Rider could do anything, Aquila had swooped through the city and plucked Garrin from the ground with her talons. The titanic trunk of Mammat attempted to swat them from the sky, but Aquila was too agile and spiralled acrobatically through the air to avoid it.

It was a time to be relieved when they reached the puffy clouds that hung over Alvoria. And as they started their flight back to Afarra, Garrin was sure he could still hear Zarad's cries of fury coming from the destruction they had left in their wake.

TWENTY-FOUR

Vassath Rider

Tallarin's training area was far more impressive than Afarra's had been. On a floor of its own in the basement of the palace, it could hold hundreds of fighters at once.

There was a fenced sparring area for those wishing to wield a sword or similar weapon, while a dozen targets were cleverly positioned at different distances along a shooting range that spanned the far wall. Elsewhere, there were wrestling mats and areas with heavy weights for those more in favour of being strong than using a weapon.

After arriving in the training area, Oracus walked around for a short time before he spotted Kivali and one of the triplets. He approached them, and Kivali offered him a warm smile when she saw him.

"It's about time," she said. "We've been waiting for you."

"I'm sorry, I got a bit lost," Oracus said.

On either side of the triplet, who Oracus assumed was Shio, the commander of Catania's army, there was a man and a woman. The man was tall with thick hair and light-brown eyes, while the woman was older with frizzy hair and yellow teeth. Kivali turned to the three. "Oracus, you remember Shio," she confirmed. "And these two are Wilos and Dyma. They're Riders too."

Oracus shook everyone's hand. "I didn't know there were more Riders here," he said.

"There are three of us in Tallarin altogether," Dyma said in a nasally voice. "Four including you."

"So what do you think of our training area, Oracus?" Shio asked.

"It's amazing," Oracus answered, looking around. "There are so many people here."

"It's nice to see it's being put to good use," Shio insisted. "But it's unfortunate a potential Jowra attack has forced so many civilians to come here."

"They all know a war is coming?" Oracus said, surprised.

"Oh yes, Catania has warned them. She's under no illusions we'll need every fighter we can find should Jowra come knocking on the wall. It's been busy like this for a number of months now."

"What training will we be doing today?" Oracus asked eagerly.

"Well, I'm sure it'll come as no surprise your training will be slightly different to that of everyone else in here. Riders have a larger variety of skills that need developing," Shio said. "So first things first, why don't we all share our powers."

"I can teleport," Kivali answered first.

"I can turn invisible," Wilos added.

"And I can create shields to protect myself," Dyma said with a shrug.

"I can copy the powers of other Riders," Oracus finished.

The reaction of Wilos and Dyma was not at all what

Oracus was expecting. They both drew their swords and pointed them at him.

"You're a Vassath?" Wilos growled fiercely.

Oracus took a fearful step backwards. "A what?"

"A Vassath Rider!" Dyma clarified, equally as fierce. "You can use more than one power?"

Shio stepped in front of Wilos and Dyma. "Both of you put your swords down. He's not a threat."

Reluctantly, they both acquiesced, but neither of them took their eyes off Oracus.

"A Vassath Rider is an unusual thing, Oracus," Shio informed. "It makes you very powerful and extremely dangerous."

Oracus was taken aback. "I'm not powerful or dangerous!" he argued. He looked to Kivali to back him up. "I can't even use my power properly."

"But with a bit of training, you will be able to," Shio said. "And you will be stronger than any other Rider in Tallarin."

"Why is that a problem?" Oracus said.

"Because the only other Vassath Rider in the whole of Pharia is Jowra himself."

Oracus gasped, and the fire in the eyes of Wilos and Dyma grew worse.

"Now do you see why your power should concern us?" Shio concluded.

"Well, yes," Oracus agreed. "But I'm nothing like Jowra."

"Jowra's soldiers killed Oracus's father," Kivali said. "He isn't likely to switch sides any time soon."

"None of us said he would."

"But Wilos and Dyma are looking at me like they think I'll cut off their heads or something," Oracus pointed out.

Shio flashed Wilos and Dyma a warning glance. "They won't doubt you any longer. And they will treat you just as they would anyone else."

Oracus looked the two Riders in the eyes. They seemed to have calmed their expressions somewhat. "I didn't ask for this power, I didn't even ask to be a Rider," he reasoned. "I don't want you to judge me for something I can't control."

Shio placed a hand on Oracus's shoulder. "I'm sorry we all reacted in such an unfair manner. We should really be celebrating a Rider who is capable of equalling Jowra's power."

Oracus frowned. "There are other Riders who are stronger than I am," he challenged.

"Yet none with your potential," Shio insisted. "But come now, maybe we should train a while. All this talk of powers is far too serious."

A minute later, the four Riders and Shio were standing inside the fenced sparring area. Shio had paired Oracus and Kivali together, as had seemed wise, and Oracus held his father's sword in his hand, with the green emerald in the hilt shining up at him.

Kivali made it her mission to prove to Wilos and Dyma that Oracus wasn't the threat they thought he was. In twenty minutes, she didn't yield to Oracus once, yet Oracus felt like he'd been in a fist-fight with a Lisor. As they fought, he noticed crowds of onlookers building around their group, and wondered if they knew he was a Rider too, or if they thought he was a normal Human receiving a punishment.

The sparring went on for another two hours, during which Shio proved why Catania thought so highly of him.

His knowledge of combat was so vast he even put Karvan of Thessley to shame. He worked on Oracus's positioning and balance, and then altered his technique so his shielding and attacking were more efficient. Then, when it came to his sword, Shio seemed to know more about it than Oracus did, and the old man hadn't even held it. He advised Oracus on where to position it, how to grip it with one hand and two, and the most effective place to strike at an opponent's body. Every minor adjustment was something Oracus hadn't even considered when sparring in the past, but such alterations made the sword feel lighter and the movements seem easier. By the end of the session, Oracus had been taught so much he saw a substantial rise in his victories over Kivali.

"Before you all leave," Shio said as Oracus slid his sword into the sheath on his belt. "I'd like you all to practise using your powers," Shio said.

Oracus felt Wilos and Dyma's eyes upon him again, and he tried his best to ignore them.

"Dyma, shield yourself," Shio demanded. He grabbed at Oracus's waist and pulled his sword free.

As he thrust the sword at her, a transparent red orb appeared around her body and blocked the blade.

"Remember what I told you," Shio reminded her as he swung Oracus's sword at the orb several more times. "The more compact your shield, the stronger it becomes."

Dyma decreased the size of the orb until it was barely large enough to contain her. Her fists were clenched, and her eyes were focused, but the shield still began to crack under Shio's onslaught.

"Kivali, get ready!" Shio bellowed.

He turned away from Dyma and swung Oracus's sword at Kivali's head. Kivali vanished instantly and the sword cut through the air where she'd been standing. She reappeared behind Shio, who twisted around and swiped at her again. For a second time, Kivali teleported just in time to dodge the blade and Shio cried out joyfully.

"Brilliant, well done!" he shouted. "Now it's your turn, Wilos."

He rounded on Wilos and advanced towards him, but Wilos used his power to vanish from sight. Shio aimed a strike at where Wilos had been standing, but there was a clang as the invisible Rider blocked the attack with his own sword. Before Shio could strike again, the sword was pulled from his grip and tossed to the ground. Wilos then reappeared with a victorious smile on his face.

"Oh, that was great!" Shio said with a laugh. Then he picked up the sword and roared, "Oracus!"

The sword was thrown at Oracus with such precision it would have pierced him between the eyes. In the moment he had to react, however, he snapped his focus onto Kivali's mind and attempted to teleport away. He felt himself start to spin, but in his panic, he lost concentration, and the force of the power propelled him away from the sword, but threw him into the metal fence. Somewhere inside himself, Oracus felt a horrible crunch, and all the air was knocked out his lungs.

"Are you okay?" Shio asked him.

Oracus nodded, "Just a bit winded."

As Shio helped him regain his feet, a huge round of applause erupted from the crowd that had gathered.

"I think you need to practise that a bit more before we try

it again," Shio advised as Oracus limped over to his sword. "But at least our audience enjoyed the show."

TWENTY-FIVE

Visions And Evil Grandfathers

"Is it him?" the deep voice rasped.

"No."

"You forget I am in your mind, Catania. I know when you're lying."

"It isn't!" Catania enforced, trying without success to hide her weakness.

"He looks like you though, don't you think?"

Catania shook her head helplessly, desperation seeping from her pores like the tears from her eyes. She leaned on the white dresser beneath the mirror and stared at her reflection. Her hair wasn't Princess-like anymore, it was as messy as when she'd been held captive in Melzor. Her skin was dry and flaky, and it itched as terribly as her muscles ached. And her eyes were no longer their usual colour, but a fiery crimson instead.

"Don't you like the way you look?" the voice provoked.

Catania lifted a marble ornament off the dresser and smashed the mirror into a thousand glittering pieces. Immediately, blood as red as her eyes began to run down her arms. "I just want you to leave me alone!" she cried.

"But we made an agreement," the voice reasoned. "You cannot go back on your word."

"But I can't keep doing this," Catania argued. "It's betrayal."

"Betrayal?" the voice repeated fiercely. "Betrayal was when you left Melzor. Betrayal was when you built an army to oppose mine. Betrayal was when you killed hundreds of my men in an attempt to dethrone me!"

Catania clutched her head as the intensity of the voice rose inside her skull.

"The boy is a Rider too, is he not?"

"No," she denied.

"Do not lie to me!" the voice thundered, its power enough to make her bones tremor.

"Okay, he is," Catania conceded.

"And does he know he's your son?"

"You've watched him through my eyes. You can see he doesn't know."

The voice remained silent for a few seconds, as if in thought. Then it spoke on, "I want you to tell him."

Catania sobbed. "Why would you want me to do that?"

"Because he will be desperate to get to know you," the voice explained. "And when he spends time with you, I will begin to understand him."

"Understand him for what purpose?"

"He's my grandchild, Catania. Must I have a reason?"

"You do nothing unless its for your own gain."

The voice cackled evilly. "Maybe I would like to build his trust so he can help me to rule this land. Perhaps he would be more willing than you were."

"I doubt that," Catania argued.

"Then I would force him to assist me," the voice said nonchalantly. "Do you know what his power is?"

"No, I don't."

"I sense you're lying to me again."

"I just told you I don't know."

"WHAT IS HIS POWER?" The voice came so loud and harsh Catania felt like her head might explode, and she threw her hands up to cover her ears.

"He can copy the powers of other Riders," she yielded.

"He can *what*?"

"You heard me," Catania said tersely.

"Oh, my, my, my!" the voice said, unable to suppress its obvious glee. "Catania, why did you keep this a secret from me?"

Catania's stomach churned inside her, and a sickness suddenly rose to her throat.

"My grandson is a Vassath Rider," the voice summarised excitedly. "This changes *everything*!"

"It changes nothing because he still won't join you," Catania denied.

"Oh, you misunderstand me, my daughter. I can't let him join me if he's a Vassath Rider, he would be far too strong. I must have his power for myself!"

"No, you can't kill him!" Catania pleaded.

"Of course I can. I've killed family for a power once before, Catania. I'm more than capable of doing it again."

"But he's my son!"

"And that is desperately unfortunate," the voice claimed. "But it is an unforgiving world, and I cannot pass up an opportunity like this."

*

Oracus bolted upright and wrestled with the sheets of his bed. When his feet swung down to the floor, he breathed deeply and wiped away the cold sweat that had gathered on his forehead.

"Bandor, wake up," he said sharply. *"I've just had another dream about Catania."*

Bandor stirred and lifted his head. *"What happened?"*

Oracus worriedly recited the conversation he'd heard in the dream. Then he sat in silence, before eventually adding, *"But there's no way I can be Catania's son."*

"How can you be sure you aren't?" Bandor contended.

"Because I lived in a little village that nobody outside Thessley knew of, and so did my father. How would he have met the Princess of Tallarin?"

"I don't know," Bandor answered. *"But can you prove he didn't?"*

Oracus considered his Lavorian's argument and quickly realised he couldn't. *"Okay, so what if I am Catania's son?"* he asked. *"What happens then?"*

"Other than you being the next in line to lead Tallarin, you mean?" Bandor said. *"Well, you now know who your mother is..."*

The words hit Oracus like a hammer to the chest. He stood up, and then started pacing the room.

"Are you alright?" Bandor asked him.

"I just need to think for a moment," he said.

"Could you perhaps ask her if it's true?" Bandor proposed.

"Not if she's being manipulated by Jowra. I don't think it would be wise for him to find out I know."

"So you intend to keep it a secret?"

"I don't have any other choice. We either keep it to ourselves, or we get Catania killed." Oracus put his face in his hands and hoped for a brilliant solution to present itself. But the only thought he had was one that troubled him further. *"If she is my mother then it makes me the grandchild of the evillest man in Pharia."*

"That doesn't make you evil too, Oracus," Bandor dismissed.

Oracus recalled his conversation with Shio about how he and Jowra were the only two Vassath Riders in Pharia. But that wasn't all that connected them; it seemed they shared the same blood too.

"We're in a difficult position now," Oracus stated. *"We can't speak about it, but if we don't then Jowra will continue to control Catania. What do we do?"*

"Kivali is your only option," Bandor said. *"You need to tell her and trust she'll know what to do."*

"You think it's a good idea to share these dreams, even with her?" Oracus asked uncertainly.

"This is bigger than the judgement you'll receive for having a few strange dreams, Oracus," Bandor said. *"The integrity of Tallarin is breached, and I don't think we're entitled to withhold what we know. We need to tell her right away."*

Dawn had barely arrived when Oracus and Bandor walked together through the dark, empty corridors of the palace. Fortunately, it appeared Sashtrams worked throughout the night, and one particularly fat Sashtram was willing to direct Oracus to the room where Kivali slept.

When Oracus knocked on her door, it took a minute for her to answer, and when she did, her dark hair was all over her face.

"This is far too early," she said sleepily.

"Any chance I can come in?" Oracus replied. "It's quite important."

Kivali stepped aside and let Oracus and Bandor inside. In the corner of the room, Onca lifted her head off her paws to watch them. When Oracus sat down on the bed, Kivali sat down beside him, and he began to tell her about the dreams.

"*Quite* important?" Kivali said as he finished. By now, she was wide awake and Onca was also out the corner she'd been sleeping in. "This is very, very serious!"

"It was actually these dreams that made me want to travel here with you from Afarra," Oracus admitted. "I knew I couldn't ignore them."

"You should have told me straight away."

"But I hardly knew you, and I didn't know what they meant," Oracus tried to justify. "Until I got here and discovered the real Catania looks exactly like the one in my dreams, I had no reason to say anything. You'd have thought I was crazy."

Kivali ran her fingers through her hair. "We need to talk to the triplets," she said. "They'll know what to do."

"But they're Catania's advisers," Oracus argued.

"And they'll do what is best for Tallarin," Kivali stated. "They're reliable and smart. That's why they're Catania's advisers."

"But Catania's life is at risk here," Oracus said.

"Farlog is far wiser than anybody else I know," Kivali forced. "I'd trust him with my life, and you should trust him with Catania's."

Oracus nodded. "When shall we speak to them then?"

"Now," Kivali insisted. "While everyone's still in bed. We don't want anyone knowing we're holding secret meetings."

Bandor and Onca stayed behind while Oracus and Kivali went off the see the triplets in Croij's laboratory. Before long, Oracus was recounting his dreams again, while the three men listened quietly and each looked down their crooked nose at him.

It was difficult for Oracus to concentrate on his stories in the laboratory. All around him, different liquids in glass vials bubbled and smoked, while mysterious objects made strange noises. At one point, a Sashtram waddled past complaining about how a three handled sword was 'stupid', and another lost both eyebrows when something it was testing exploded.

"Forgive me for appearing rude, but your tale is very hard to believe," Croij said when Oracus finished speaking. "I've never heard of anyone who can do what you claim to do."

Oracus turned to Kivali. "I knew this was a bad idea."

"On the contrary, it would have been a mistake not to discuss this with us," Farlog said. "I agree it appears farfetched, but I can't say I'd have wanted this information to go unheard."

"You believe me?" Oracus said with surprise.

"May I ask you a question before I pass judgement?"

Oracus shrugged. "I guess so."

"Have you ever had a dream like this that wasn't of either Catania or Jowra?"

Oracus looked seriously at Farlog. "When we were in Lalacia, I read some text in a book about a man called King

Xarmoud. I then had a dream about him too."

"King Xarmoud?" Shio said. "The King who sacrificed himself to end the Noble War?"

"Oracus is Visioning," Farlog explained as he rubbed his chin in thought. "His dreams are not just simple dreams."

"What is Visioning?" Kivali asked.

"It's a power that allows someone to see events that happened in the past, and to sometimes see what's happening in the present."

"A power?" Croij followed up. "But Oracus already has a power."

"A power to copy the powers of others," Shio reminded. "Is there another Rider here in Tallarin who Oracus is copying?"

"I don't think this power has anything to do with being a Rider," Farlog said. "I believe it is something only Oracus can do. And I suspect he could do it before he even became a Rider."

"I wasn't a Rider when I dreamt of Catania being chased through the forest by Jowra's soldiers," Oracus confirmed.

Croij looked blankly at Oracus, and then turned back to Farlog. "But that's impossible," he disputed. "There's never been a power seen in anyone but a Rider."

"What about the Hazinals?" Farlog claimed. "Would you not say they have powers?"

"The Hazinals are a myth!"

"Do you have any proof?"

"It's common knowledge, I don't need proof."

Despite having his every point contended, Farlog offered a smile. "I do have a theory on all this. But until I've done some research, I cannot speak with any real accuracy."

"But you believe me?" Oracus said.

"This would be a very extravagant and well-constructed lie if it were one," Farlog said. "And you don't strike me as the duplicitous sort."

"So the threat to Tallarin is real?" Shio questioned concernedly.

"Of that I have no doubt," Farlog said.

"Then what do we do?"

"Firstly, we must keep what we have discussed a secret. We cannot let Catania find out, should it cause us a more substantial problem," Farlog insisted. "Secondly, we must hope Jowra allows us time to prepare our weapon."

"Our weapon?" Oracus questioned.

"You!" Farlog stated. "It is you, Oracus, who can compete with him. Not only do you have the power of a Vassath Rider, but you have the power to spy on his plans too. You are the key to this war. You are our glimmer of hope."

"But I thought you'd all hate me for claiming I'm his grandson," Oracus contested.

"We are still wary of you," Croij said.

Farlog shook his head seriously. "No. You may be his grandson, which could be seen as a reason to distrust you. But you can also be his downfall, and that is far more important."

TWENTY-SIX

A Walk And A Kiss

The next few weeks were a blur.

After Farlog had suggested Oracus may be the difference in the war, Oracus began to train with more focus and desire than ever. If Tallarin needed him to be their *weapon*, he would ensure he had complete control over his power, and he would train until he was as prolific with a sword as he could be. If he could prove his commitment to the rebellion, then maybe the likes of Wilos, Dyma, Croij and Quent would be more accepting of him too, and less likely to believe he would stab them in the back.

So all his time was spent either practising his power, wielding his sword, or shooting his bow at targets in the training area, while he relentlessly exercised his connection with Bandor's mind. Kivali and Shio were the perfect partner and tutor during sparring sessions, and Oracus learned more in a few weeks than he had throughout the rest of his life.

And because of their endless time spent together, Oracus and Kivali's relationship reached new heights. Oracus had never felt so comfortable with someone, not even Garrin, and he woke up each morning with an eagerness to get to the training area and see her.

On a day when the rain fell and the training area under the palace was heaving with civilians who had nothing better to do, Oracus found Kivali's hip with a particularly quick strike of his sword. She cried out in pain, but hit back with a thrust of her own that nearly found Oracus's gut. Oracus teleported away and Kivali followed him, and they traded more blows that echoed off the high ceiling.

"Know when to retreat and when to hold your ground!" Shio's shout came loud and clear, and Oracus took several steps backwards.

As Kivali advanced towards him, Oracus asked her a question he had been meaning to for some time. "Would you like to take a walk with me tonight?" he suggested.

"A walk?" she asked, not hesitating and aiming a fast attack at his shoulder.

Oracus blocked the strike and then evaded the next. "It doesn't matter," he said nervously. "Forget I said anything."

"Where to?" she probed with interest, stepping forwards again.

"I don't know. Around the city maybe."

"You-mean-like-as-a-date?" She thrust at him with each word she spoke.

"Well, I mean, I guess so," Oracus said sheepishly as he offered his own attack.

Kivali squatted low beneath Oracus's sword and swiped his legs from under him. He landed hard on his back, and she planted her foot on his chest. A gentle smile crossed her face. "I would really like to go for a walk with you," she said happily.

Later that day, Oracus knocked on the door to Kivali's room in the palace. For the first time in a while, he had tried to comb his hair.

"Hold on," came her voice from the other side.

When the door opened, Oracus's mouth dropped open. Kivali was wearing a blue dress that matched her eyes, and it embraced her body perfectly. Her sparkling blue shoes helped her stand a few inches taller and her dark hair was full of curls.

Oracus kissed her on the cheek. "You look amazing," he said.

"That's very kind of you to say," she replied. "You look pretty good yourself."

"I thought we could go to the workshop before our walk," Oracus suggested. "I know you're probably used to it, but I quite enjoy watching the Sashtrams at work."

Kivali agreed and they strolled together along the corridor until they reached the staircase. When Kivali linked her arm in Oracus's, goosepimples rose on his skin.

"You've never really told me much about your life in Thessley," she said in a voice that was as soft as her warm skin.

"I don't really have much to say about it," Oracus said truthfully. "It was peaceful. And the people there were friendly."

"What did you do there?" Kivali went on. "I mean, what did you like to do to pass the time?"

"I used to go hunting in the forest," Oracus said. "My father hated the forest so I'd always go in alone. It was nice to get away sometimes and think about what might be *out there.*"

"Out there? Beyond the forest, you mean?"

"I had a book at home called *'Beasts of Legend'*, and I used to pretend I was searching for the beasts when I was in the forest," Oracus said with a laugh. "It was difficult to imagine what was beyond the trees though, because I'd never seen cities or mountains or desert. My father always told me I was too curious when I asked him if the beasts in the book were real."

"What was your father like?"

Oracus smiled sadly. Just being asked the question brought back memories of him rocking in his chair by the fire. There was a scent of tobacco that came with it too, like his father was right behind them, listening in on their conversation. "He was a really great man," Oracus said. "He made me who I am today."

"He would be proud of how you've handled all this."

"I hope so."

"Did he ever speak about your mother?" Kivali asked.

"Never openly," Oracus said. "I asked him sometimes, but he would just say she was a wonderful woman and that her reason for leaving us had been a good one. And I believed him."

They reached the door to the workshop and could hear the noise of the machines before they'd even entered. Kivali looked at Oracus and offered him a rueful smile. "Are you okay?"

"I'm fine," Oracus assured. "I miss him but it's over now. I can't bring him back, so I just have to keep moving forwards."

The Sashtrams were all busy doing one thing or another

when they walked inside. Some were servicing the machines, while others scribbled results on paper. One even held his friend by the ankles and dangled him inside a huge vat of gloop in an attempt to retrieve his pencil. It was evening, but the tiny creatures with blue skin were all still hard at work.

"Do you find it tough having to live here in limbo?" Oracus asked as he looked around with interest. "We're preparing for a day that may never come. Jowra may never attack."

"I've lived my whole life like this, Oracus. I'm used to it," Kivali answered.

"Have you ever tried to imagine what it would be like if we won the war?"

"You know, success frightens me more than the war itself," Kivali said. "I get up in the morning now to train, and to prepare myself for the day he arrives with his army. But if we won, what would drive me forwards? What would be my purpose?"

The answer was quite a sad one, Oracus thought, but it held merit too. Ordinarily, he would have advocated peace, but he had been guilty of wishing for more when he'd had peace in Thessley. Maybe there was something boring about peace. "You could come hunting with me in the forest," was all he could think to say.

They watched the Sashtrams quietly for a while longer. Thoughts of Jowra and his father briefly left Oracus's mind as he chuckled at the Sashtrams and their strange ways. When a few minutes had passed, a serious-looking Sashtram with a bushy beard walked past and tripped over its own cloak. It fell heavily, but jumped up quickly and brushed itself down, hoping nobody had noticed. But when Oracus and Kivali laughed, it didn't take too kindly to them, and it waved its fist threateningly in their direction.

"I think that's our cue to leave," Kivali said with a smirk.

With the Sashtram still glowering at them, they exited the workshop and walked through the entrance hall towards the door that led out into the city. When they appeared on the palace steps, the city seemed to come to a halt before them. It was eerily quiet, and the streets were desolate but for a cat that prowled in the shadows. The evening brought a thickening darkness, but there was a certain romance in the orange sun dropping beyond the wall in the distance. There was little romance, however, in the odour of sewage that rose from the drains.

Oracus and Kivali walked down the steps and began their stroll through the streets that would take them to the far side of the city.

"So what's the deal with Catania and Alticon?" Oracus asked as they passed between towering buildings that blocked out what little sunlight remained. "They're no longer Rider and Lavorian, right?"

"They haven't been for a few years," Kivali answered.

"Do you know what happened to them?"

"Jowra killed Catania and their bond was broken."

"Jowra killed her? But that's impossible!" Oracus said.

"Catania's power was to revive the dead," Kivali explained. "When he killed her, he inherited her power and then used it to bring her back to life."

"He did *what*?"

"It's abhorrent, isn't it?" Kivali said with a shake of her

head. "And that's why Alticon has no armour too."

"Do you think there's anything Jowra wouldn't do for power?"

"No, I don't," Kivali replied seriously. "Do you remember me telling you that Jowra used the armour of Lavorians to build a second Dragon?" She waited for Oracus to nod. "Well, rumour has it that Alticon's armour was the final piece of that Dragon. Pseubas was created on the same day Catania was killed."

Just the thought of it made Oracus feel sick. "In my latest dream of Catania, Jowra told her he wanted to kill me for my power," he disclosed. "He also said he'd killed family before. I didn't realise he meant her."

Kivali nodded. "If Jowra killed you then we really wouldn't stand a chance. If he could copy the power of any Rider fighting against him then he'd be unstoppable."

Oracus relived that part of his dream in his mind. He wondered if Jowra would consider reviving him, or if he'd just leave him to rot.

"Imagine being betrayed like that by your own father," Oracus said. "It's no wonder she built an army to fight against him."

"Yet if we assume your dreams are real, we know he's blackmailing her now to get what he needs. He's a man who should never be given power, so it makes sense we should take it away from him."

When Oracus and Kivali reached the wall, night had truly fallen. The sun had vanished, and the stars were twinkling brightly on a clear sky. Still the streets were clear. They hadn't seen a single soul except a few patrolling soldiers and a young lamp-lighter. That was until a shout split the silence and a familiar face came out of the darkness nearby.

"Morpac!" Oracus exclaimed with surprise. The man they had saved from the Grevlors and Lisors in the mountains looked much healthier than when they'd last seen him. He was clean for a start, and he no longer had bruising around his eye. And he also wore an expensive purple cloak with a high collar. "You look fantastic."

"Yer very kind," Morpac replied with a bow. He shook Oracus's hand vigorously, and then kissed Kivali's hand lightly. "A face tha' could start another war," he said to her. "An' yer 'av skills tha' could probably end wars too!"

"Not this war though, unfortunately," Kivali replied.

"Yer will in time," Morpac assured. He then took a step back from them. "Yer mus' come with me. Uswir would love ter see yer. An' the shop too. It's marvellous."

Morpac was soon leading them through alleys and streets between the buildings of Tallarin. They stayed near to the wall, which remained huge and intimidating above them, and eventually reached a small square with a weapon stall at its heart. Standing alone at the stall was Uswir. Since returning to Tallarin, his hair and beard had been combed, and he'd gained a lot of weight.

As the three of them approached, he looked up and offered a gleaming smile. "Ahhh. Welcome, friends!"

The stall was stacked with daggers and knives, and a few swords and bows hung in the roof above Uswir's head. Behind Uswir, the open doorway of a flat stone building offered a glance into what appeared to be their workshop.

"Business is thrivin' 'ere," Uswir said proudly. "Since we came 'ome, we've been makin' weapons fer the soldiers."

"Shio 'imself came 'ere to ask us on Princess Catania's be'alf," Morpac explained. "Apparently, the Sastrams couldn't keep up, so they needed our 'elp."

"It looks great," Oracus said of the stall as he picked up a dagger with an elegant blade and a black handle.

"It's yours if yer wan' it," Uswir offered. "Free o' charge."

"Oh no, I can't do that," Oracus refused.

"Yer saved our lives in the mountains. One dagger doesn't come close ter 'ow much we owe yer." Morpac took the dagger and slotted it into Oracus's belt. "Easy ter conceal, see. An' good fer stabbin' a Grevlor with if they try ter make yer their prisoner!"

"Thank you," Oracus said gratefully.

"Ye'r very welcome." Morpac shook Oracus's hand again. "Now, let's show yer the workshop. Yer'll like it in there."

Oracus and Kivali spent an hour with Morpac and Uswir before they made their excuses and left. Before long, their walk was over, and they were back inside the palace with the smell of waste thankfully behind them.

Oracus accompanied Kivali back to her quarters, where she slowly opened the door. "That was a very nice walk," she said. "Thank you for asking me."

"Thank you for saying yes," Oracus replied. "It was much better *with* company than it would have been *without*."

Kivali turned back to face Oracus. "Maybe we could do it again soon?"

"I'd like that," Oracus said.

Kivali looked softly at him and he struggled to hold her gaze. He shuffled his feet awkwardly and glanced along the empty corridor.

"Aren't you going to kiss me?" she asked.

Oracus felt his cheeks flush. When he looked back at Kivali, her eyes were like pools of water waiting for him to dive in. He still couldn't hold her gaze, so he closed his eyes and took an anxious step forwards.

It felt like he was standing in that corridor for an eternity. But when Kivali's lips finally met with his, every concern in his head seemed to exist no more.

TWENTY-SEVEN

Chiming Bell

Jowra swept his long, greasy hair from his eyes as fury coursed through his veins. He marched purposefully through the darkness with his black cloak billowing behind him and the cold snow crunching under his feet.

The magnificence of the palace in Melzor was unparalleled, but even walking up its icy steps did nothing to quell Jowra's rage. A Grevlor at the palace door offered him a respectful bow as he passed. But with an indignant sneer, Jowra struck the Grevlor across the face with a pale hand, leaving it whimpering in his wake.

Jowra swept through the palace to the room he cherished most – the keep. The keep was colossal; never had there been a room so grand. The four walls reached far and wide, and they rose not to a ceiling, but to an open view of the night's sky. Snowflakes fell inside the keep, onto a floor that was already a foot deep in white powder. It was so cold and blustery that the oil lamps on the walls refused to light.

Inside the keep, two enormous Dragon Lavorians were waiting for him, their silver bodies reflecting the moonlight. They were lying on the snow, their long bodies entwined like rope, and still they were several metres tall.

"My King," they rasped together, breathing smoke out their nostrils and bowing their heads.

Both Lavorians – Wravias and Pseubas – had crimson eyes like their Rider. Their jaws were full of sword-sized teeth, and from the crown of their armoured heads to the tips of their armoured tails, they were covered in sharp silver spines.

"Where is Zarad?" Jowra asked as soon as his Lavorians were in sight.

"Riskin is bringing him here," Wravias answered.

As if Wravias's words were a cue, two men followed Jowra into the keep. One was short and clumsy, while the other tall and handsome.

The shorter of the men spoke first in a fearful mumble, "My King, we have a guest."

"I am well aware of that, Riskin," Jowra replied, attempting to suppress his impatience.

The second man, Zarad, walked arrogantly forwards. He lowered himself casually onto one knee. "My King," he said smoothly.

"Stand up and explain yourself!" Jowra demanded, unable to stop his fury from enveloping him.

Zarad stood and his expression quickly changed. "Alvoria was attacked, my King."

"Do not consider me a fool, Zarad! My only foolishness was trusting someone with your incompetence!" The walls of the keep shook under the might of Jowra's voice. "Alvoria wasn't merely attacked, it was burned to the ground!"

"It was an unfortunate event," Zarad said quietly.

"*Unfortunate* suggests it was down to chance," Jowra disputed. "But I specifically remember telling you that Alvoria was vulnerable and that I needed you to protect it. What went wrong?"

Zarad gathered himself but couldn't conceal his fear. "A Rider from the rebellion attacked while I was absent, my King."

"Absent for what purpose?" Jowra probed, now pacing angrily.

Zarad dropped his eyes guiltily to the floor. "I had no reason, my King."

"But you returned to Alvoria in time to apprehend the culprit?" Jowra pressed.

"I returned when the city was already on fire," Zarad replied. "There was nothing I could do."

"And you apprehended the culprit?" Jowra repeated.

"No, my King. The Rider and his Lavorian got away."

"GOT AWAY?" The ferocity of Jowra's voice knocked Zarad off his feet. Riskin quickly covered his ears and the two Dragons shirked away from the noise.

"I didn't mean for it to happen," Zarad claimed.

"It was just one Rider and he destroyed an entire city of mine," Jowra summarised, breathing deeply to control his voice. "You have allowed them to make a mockery of my reign."

"I'm sorry, my King. It won't happen again. I promise."

"You have really disappointed me, Zarad. And there must be consequences," Jowra said. "Riskin, stand over there by that wall."

Riskin ran obediently to where Jowra was pointing,

leaving Zarad alone and frightened.

Jowra took several steps away from Zarad and then turned to the Dragons. "Pseubas, burn him!" he commanded aloud.

The Dragons slithered apart, and the smaller of the two moved forwards, its large claws scraping the stone floor. It lifted its head and filled its chest with air, before letting out a jet of flames that passed by Zarad and engulfed Riskin instead.

There wasn't even a scream to hear as Riskin was killed, nor was there anything that remained of him except the scorch mark on the wall where he'd been standing. There was only a moment of bright light and intense warmth in the keep before the cold darkness returned.

"I have a legion of soldiers beneath this palace waiting to be commanded," Jowra said, his voice now much calmer than it had been. "I want you to march with them to Tallarin where you will join Gravaz's forces in destroying the wall and leaving the city as nothing more than rubble beneath your feet. Am I understood?"

Zarad had tears on his cheeks he was so relieved to be alive. "Yes, my King," he said.

Jowra made to leave the keep. But before he reached the door, he looked back at the black mark on the wall. "Zarad," he said. "Don't fail me this time."

*

"Kivali!" Oracus shouted as his knuckles rapped on her door. "Kivali!"

When Kivali opened the door, her expression was

serious. "He's coming, isn't he?"

"Two armies are on their way," Oracus confirmed. "We need to talk to the triplets!"

Oracus recited his latest dream to Kivali and the triplets in Croij's laboratory. Bandor and Onca were there too, and there was a solemn atmosphere when he finished.

"And you're sure you didn't misinterpret this dream?" Croij questioned concernedly.

"It sounds to me like there was nothing to misinterpret," Farlog said. "If Alvoria was attacked then it would provoke Jowra to retaliate."

"But Torvanon agreed not to attack any of Jowra's cities," Kivali reminded. "Why would he go back on his word?"

"Without having contact with Torvanon, it's difficult to predict what might have happened since you held counsel with him in Afarra. They may have been attacked themselves, or maybe one of their Riders went rogue."

"What matters now is how much time we have to mount a defence," Shio expressed.

"Unfortunately, our guess isn't likely to be very precise," Farlog responded. "The timing of Visioning is inaccurate. Oracus's dream may have happened tonight, or it may have happened a week ago."

"So Jowra's soldiers may have the wall in their sights right now?" Croij proposed.

"It's a possibility, yes," Farlog answered.

"Then I need to ready our defence right now," Shio stated. "Kivali, can you alert Wilos and Dyma of what we know?"

Kivali and Onca left the laboratory with Shio, leaving Oracus and Bandor with Farlog and Croij.

"You're certain Jowra isn't joining the attack?" Farlog checked, looking seriously at Oracus.

"He's definitely staying in Melzor," Oracus replied. "He has sent Gravaz and Zarad."

Farlog sighed. "Then that leaves us with some hope, at least."

"What happens now?" Oracus asked.

"You need to help organise the soldiers and keep the families calm," Farlog said. "Go and find Kivali, she'll tell you what to do."

Oracus and Bandor left the laboratory in quiet haste. They descended staircases and traversed corridors that led them to the palace entrance hall. On every level of the palace, Sashtrams were already knocking on doors and warning those inside. Soon, there were shouts of panic ringing in the walls.

"All this because of a dream," Oracus said gloomily.

"It may be the most important dream you ever have," Bandor replied.

Oracus and Bandor found Kivali beside the statue in the entrance hall. Wilos and Dyma were already with her, and the two Riders looked sternly at Oracus when he approached.

Oracus ignored them and spoke directly to Kivali, "Farlog told me to help you. What do you need me to do?"

"We need to warn everyone of what's coming. Those who can fight need to arm themselves. Those who can't fight need to prepare for leaving their homes."

"Where will the children go when Jowra's army arrives?" Oracus asked worriedly.

"To the floors below the palace," Kivali answered. "There

are secret routes in here that lead to the mountains."

There was a surge of bodies inside the entrance hall and petrified people ran in every direction; some carrying weapons, others carrying children. There was a cacophony of screams and shouts, and Oracus could barely hear himself think.

"We need to calm these people somehow," Kivali said. "We all need to find an entrance and reassure everyone who passes through. This could get out of hand if we don't."

But as the four Riders were about to separate, the low chiming of a bell rang loudly over their heads. Silence and stillness fell over the palace, and everybody stood with their mouths agape and terror in their eyes.

Oracus turned to Kivali for an explanation.

"They're here," she said fearfully. "Jowra's soldiers are here!"

TWENTY-EIGHT

The Battle Of Tallarin

In the moments that followed the chime of the bell, there was eerie silence. Then pandemonium.

The noise of scared, innocent people searching for safety was deafening, and no number of Riders and Lavorians would be enough to bring order.

"What do we do?" Oracus shouted over the screams.

"There's no time to assist these people now," Kivali replied. "They know what to do when the bell rings. We must prepare ourselves for battle."

"My armour is in my room," Oracus said. "And so is my sword."

"Then don your armour and retrieve your sword," Kivali ordered. "I'll see you at the wall."

Oracus wasted no time. In minutes, he was bundling through the door to his quarters with Bandor close behind him. Inside, he quickly acquired his armour, which was as blue as the sky – except today the sky outside his window was full of dark clouds; it seemed even the weather felt Tallarin's misery. When Oracus's sword and dagger were sheathed at his belt, and his quiver, bow and shield were hanging over his shoulders, he left the palace and headed through the streets towards the wall. The rain began to fall on Tallarin, and the smell of waste rose from the sewers like never before.

It took Oracus a long time to reach the wall. The streets of Tallarin were unrecognisable under the shadow of war. He had to push through frightened families who were running for the shelter of the palace, and past soldiers who didn't know whether to help the innocents or assemble for battle. At the wall, thousands of soldiers looked exactly as Oracus did. Blue armour beneath a grey sky and a black wall. They stood side by side, rows and rows of them, and more joined the ranks as time went on.

Kivali and Onca were at the very base of the wall facing the troops. They stood with Wilos and Dyma and their two Lavorians, inspiring the fighters with their presence. Wilos's Lavorian was called Edinuc, a Rhino the size of Onca. Huadlan was an Orangutan, the smallest Lavorian Oracus had met, and his arms wrapped around Dyma's neck like a scarf.

"This is really happening, isn't it?" he said as he strode towards them.

There was a rumble of noise that sounded like thunder.

"I can hear Jowra's forces marching across the sand," Kivali noted. "They're almost here."

"Are we ready?" Oracus asked.

"Shio is organising the archers on the wall. He's in that tower." Kivali pointed to the watchtower that stood on the top of the wall. "I doubt it will be long before we fire on them."

"Can I go up there?"

"Be my guest," Kivali returned. "But you won't like what you see."

Alone, Oracus climbed the stairs inside the wall. It took him almost ten minutes to ascend the wall, and another five to reach the top of the watchtower. There, Shio stood with a handful of his finest archers, and all along the battlements below them were hundreds more.

Oracus unhooked his bow from his shoulder and offered Shio a light nod. "I guess this is what you trained us for," he said.

"Yet I always hoped the day would never come," Shio replied. "It's quite an army he's sent."

Oracus looked beyond the balustrade at the world beneath, and gasped. Left and right there were slopes leading to mountains, but in front there was nothing but sand. On the sand, a force marched forwards in a spectacular formation that was almost as intimidating as its size.

A wall the height of Tallarin's seemed not to daunt an army with Mammat at the fore. The Elephant matched the wall for immensity, and it was only because Oracus stood atop the watchtower that he could look down upon the beast. On Mammat's head stood Zarad, just far enough away that Oracus couldn't see the paint on his face. And far beneath them, Gravaz and Lapsin strode forwards with urgency.

"Gravaz is still alive," Oracus said to Bandor. *"The fireball in Fervia didn't kill him."*

Behind the two Lavorians and their Riders, a vast army of red-armoured fighters proceeded in their thousands through a downpour that suddenly came from the heavens.

Huge pools collected on the battleground to Tallarin's front as the rain persisted. The Humans and Grevlors splashed through the water as they approached the wall, while the powerful Lisors dragged Jowra's catapults into range. Amongst the creatures Oracus knew of, there were others that he didn't. Faceless, hooded men glided alongside their comrades with sweeping red cloaks and a long wooden staff held in their pale hands.

"What are those things?" Oracus asked fearfully, pointing out the hooded men to Shio.

"They're Eeveks," Shio told him. "Silent mercenaries bred by Jowra solely to fight in this war."

The army that confronted Tallarin came to a halt. They were so close now that Mammat could probably have reached out and touched the wall with his trunk. The arrival of the soldiers was announced with a thousand evil battlecries, and then a repetitive, resounding thump of weapons on shields.

Shio stepped away from the balustrade that looked over Jowra's army and moved to that which overlooked his own troops. He was an ageing man, but he carried himself with such conviction that Oracus was sure he lived for war. Oracus stood beside him and looked down into Tallarin, where everyone squinted up at them through the rain, the terror expressed in their faces. Although the streets were full of men, their army was barely half of Jowra's, and many of the men were not true fighters.

Shio cleared his throat, and then addressed his army with a voice that echoed off the buildings. "Soldiers of Tallarin. The day has come that we must fight for our city, and fight for our land!" he announced. "Jowra has sent an army of thousands, hoping numbers will ensure his victory. It is true there are more of them than us, but every soldier of his is empty! We fight for our families, for our children, and for our homes, but they fight because they are scared. Scared of a King who dares not to face us himself." There was silence on the ground beneath the watchtower. "Let us show them the size of our hearts, and let us help them to endure Jowra no longer. Put them out their misery, men, and let us bring prosperity back to Pharia!"

The roar that followed was spine-tingling. Every man on the ground beat their shield with the hilt of their weapon.

"Archers, ready your arrows!" Shio ordered.

The sound of hundreds of arrows being nocked to bowstrings broke through the rain. Oracus prepared an arrow of his own and aimed it over the wall.

"Fire!"

A wave of metal arched through the air at Shio's command. Oracus lost sight of his own arrow as they all came together and dropped into Jowra's ranks as one, killing hundreds of Grevlors and Humans that were beneath them.

The first strike brought bellows of anger from the enemy, and then a dozen rocks were fired from catapults. The rocks crumbled against Tallarin's wall without leaving a mark, and the archers all cheered.

"Fire again!" Shio cried.

More arrows fell into the enemy soldiers, and a second batch of rocks did nothing the weaken the wall.

"Keep firing, men!"

Oracus loosed several arrows from his bow along with

every other archer who protected the wall. Jowra's men fell in their hundreds under the onslaught, and Oracus's heart lifted in his chest. They were going to win, he thought prematurely, and without a single enemy scaling Tallarin's wall.

Then Mammat's trunk sounded like a horn, and the enormous Elephant charged.

Oracus panicked in the few seconds that came next. He shouted to Shio that they must get off the watchtower, but there wasn't enough time for that. When the collision came, it was like being on a boat at sea. The watchtower lurched, and Oracus grabbed for anything that might steady his legs. But the fall was inevitable. The tower leaned as the stone gave way beneath it, and Oracus screamed as he felt the floor give way under his feet. Shio and the archers around Oracus tumbled too, and then they were falling to their death.

"Oracus, your power!" Bandor roared.

In the moment Oracus had to react, he found Kivali's mind and tapped into her power. He thought about Tallarin's streets as he fell, and then he disappeared.

When he opened his eyes, he was lying in a puddle a hundred yards from the wall. There was a tremendous crash near to him, and a plume of dust billowed through the city streets. The watchtower had fallen, and the wall had been damaged.

"Are you okay?" Bandor said worriedly. *"Are you hurt?"*

Oracus pushed himself to his feet. He was dazed, but he wasn't injured. *"I'm fine,"* he said. *"But what about Shio?"*

"The tower collapsed. There's no way he survived the fall.

Oracus cursed and berated himself for being so foolish.

Why hadn't he grabbed Shio before he teleported?

"I could have saved him, Bandor. I could have got him out of there!"

Oracus staggered back to where the watchtower had fallen. The dust was beginning to settle, but a hole had been opened in the wall.

"Step back from the rubble!" Kivali was shouting over the heads of the soldiers on the ground. "Focus on the breach. We need to keep their forces from entering the city!"

There was a scraping of stone on the other side of the wall, and the soldiers raised their weapons in preparation for what was coming. Dyma created a shield to block the gap, but when the enemy appeared on the other side, it wasn't long before they smashed it and came flooding into the city.

The Humans and Grevlors were first to attack, but they were overwhelmed by the sheer number of soldiers that waited for them. Arrows flew at the gap in the wall, some fired by Oracus himself, and many others were brought down by the blades of swords. The few who survived the initial defence were quickly mauled or trampled by Bandor, Onca and Edinuc.

But when the Lisors and Eeveks began to creep into the city, they were much harder for the soldiers to kill. The skin of the Lisors was as tough as any armour, and the Eeveks were agile enough to evade the arrows. When the Lisors and Eeveks came, the other fighters managed to sneak through the gap in the wall, and suddenly the battle had spilled onto the streets.

Oracus shot arrows whenever he could, and he used his

sword if the enemy came too close. But the unexpected sights and sounds of battle terrified him, and he tried to keep at a safe distance. If he ever felt he was in too much danger, he would teleport to a spot where fewer soldiers were fighting.

Meanwhile, the other Riders fought bravely in front of their comrades, slaughtering dozens of foes, including the Lisors and Eeveks. If ever they appeared in trouble, they would use their power to save themselves, or their Lavorian would make a timely intervention.

As time went on, more of Jowra's men found their way into the city. Soon, Oracus was no longer able to retreat, and the streets were too full for him to avoid the enemy. It was a position that made him very uncomfortable, and he spent most of his time hiding behind his shield.

"Oracus, we need you to fight!" Bandor implored. *"We need all the help we can get."*

"I can't bring myself to do it," Oracus answered feebly. *"I'm scared!"*

"You're a better fighter than Wilos and Dyma, and they're both doing fine. You'll be alright."

"I'll be one mistake away from getting a sword through my heart."

"You rarely make mistakes when you train with Kivali, and she's a Rider!" Bandor exclaimed impatiently. *"Just pretend you're training with her… except this time you want to cut her head off."*

"That's easier for you to say when swords can't kill you!"

"Just stay near to me and we'll both be okay. If you focus on the Lisors and Eeveks, I'll make sure no Grevlors or Humans sneak up behind you."

Oracus had no choice but to risk his life. If his own Lavorian was calling him out for his cowardice, then he was sure Wilos and Dyma were probably thinking it too. He needed to prove to them he was against Jowra, and he needed to prove to them that being a Vassath Rider didn't make him an enemy. He started to advance on the fighters around him, and he quickly brought them crashing to the ground with his sword. The Lisors were big and strong, but he was too quick for them. And the Eeveks were fast and nimble, but they could do nothing to defend themselves against a teleporting Rider.

With Oracus's confidence growing by the second, and with three other Riders dominating Jowra's assault, the forces of Tallarin were able to contain the hole in the wall. Fewer foes were making it onto the city streets, and fewer friendly troops were dying as a consequence.

"Keep pushing them back!" Kivali commanded.

From beyond the wall, Mammat's trunk bellowed for a second time, signalling defeat to Jowra's men, and then his forces began to retreat from the city.

There was cheering from the soldiers of Tallarin as the enemy fled. They lifted their swords above their heads and shouted out victoriously. Some even embraced their comrades. But there were hundreds dead. A majority wore the crimson of Jowra, but many men of blue had died too; some to swords, and others who had been crushed when the watchtower had fallen.

The rain continued to fall on Tallarin, and it washed away the blood that had been sacrificed. The patter of raindrops brought a certain serenity, but the stench of death was one that Oracus would likely never forget. But at least the battle was over, at least they could regroup and be grateful for their lives.

It was then that the screams rang out from the archers who still manned the wall. "They're not retreating!" one voice cried.

There was a thunderous crash that made the ground tremble. A hundred yards to Oracus's left, archers were thrown from the parapet atop the wall as cracks appeared on its face. A second crash came, then a third, and suddenly the wall gave way to the weight of the Elephant Lavorian that was breaking through it.

Oracus gasped as the wall fell and another cloud of dust was driven through Tallarin's streets.

"Breach!" Kivali yelled over the panic around her. "Everyone needs to defend that point!"

When Mammat withdrew from the hole he had created, a deluge of Jowra's men came through it. The Tallarin forces all moved to secure the wall, but then more soldiers came through the first breach.

"We need to keep this side occupied," Oracus said to Bandor. *"If too many soldiers get through here then our forces will be swamped."*

Bandor was quick to respond, and he swiped his claws at the Humans and Grevlors that clambered into the city. Oracus readied his bow again and fired several arrows that found their mark.

"Oh no, they're coming!" Bandor said. *"Gravaz and Lapsin are here."*

Bandor had barely uttered the words when Lapsin leaped through the gap in the wall with Gravaz saddled to his back. When the Hyena's paws met the floor, Gravaz jumped from the saddle and confronted Oracus with a twisted smile.

"We meet again," he growled.

Since Oracus had struck Gravaz with a fireball outside Fervia, his face had healed, but there was significant scarring that showed how much damage had been caused, and he wore a patch over his left eye.

"You taught me a very valuable lesson when last we met," Gravaz said. "I will not fail again."

The Ulatori's flail was in his right hand, and a flame was clasped in his left. He looked taller than he had in Fervia, and the scarring made him even more terrifying.

"We need to get away from here, Oracus," Bandor warned. *"It isn't safe."*

Gravaz raised the flame above his head and threw it at Oracus. Oracus somehow side-stepped the attack, but a second ball of fire came, and he locked onto Dyma's power and protected himself with a magical shield. A third fireball was thrown, and cracks appeared in Oracus's shield, and then the fourth created an explosion that shattered the shield and knocked him backwards.

"Kill the Lavorian!" Gravaz ordered Lapsin.

Oracus kept his focus on Gravaz but he could feel Bandor's fear increasing. Lapsin was much bigger than him, and far more powerful.

"Jowra wouldn't like it if you killed me or my Lavorian," Oracus said.

Gravaz didn't show any concern other than a brief pause mid-movement. "And why is that?" he asked.

"Because he wants my power," Oracus replied.

"I have been ordered to destroy this city. The King said

nothing about saving lives!"

Oracus felt Bandor's pain as Lapsin attacked him. There was a scuffle behind him, the sound of snarling jaws and the scaping of metal paws on the floor, but Oracus still didn't look away from Gravaz.

"Your Lavorian will die in pain and I will burn you until you squeal," Gravaz growled.

Oracus searched for Gravaz's mind and then linked to his power. He put his hand behind his back to conceal it from the Ulatori, and then felt a familiar tingle of warmth in his palm. "Then you'd better be as fast as you are big," he retaliated.

He threw the fireball at Gravaz with all his might. He expected to see Gravaz's shock, but the Ulatori dodged the fire and it shot past his face. There was an explosion on what was left of the wall behind him, and his expression twisted in hatred. "You dare to use my own power against me twice?" he bellowed.

A fireball was thrown back at Oracus. He spun around quickly and it hit the shield on his back with more force than he had expected, knocking him onto his front. In moments, the giant hand of the Ulatori had grasped his midriff and he was thrown like a child's doll into the rubble.

When he landed, Oracus hit his head and felt the world spin. Through his dizziness, he saw a flood of red entering the city through the gap in the wall he was supposed to be guarding. And near the gap, Lapsin's teeth were clamped around Bandor's leg.

Gravaz closed in again. This time, the Ulatori swung the metal ball of his flail around his body expertly. There was a maniacal grin on his hideous face. "Time to die," he snarled.

The first blow of the flail smashed rock as Oracus rolled out of the way. But the second caught his arm and drew a scream of pain that he couldn't hold in. Blood spilled from the wound and Gravaz smiled wickedly, knowing he was near to victory. The Ulatori made circles with the flail and Oracus could hear nothing but the whirring it made; it was terrifying. The moment that spiky, metal ball came down would be his last.

"You'll never beat him with weapons," Bandor advised, his words filled with the pain Lapsin was causing him. *"Keep using your power."*

Gravaz was preparing to end Oracus's life. The flail hummed through the air with more and more speed, until the Ulatori raised it above his head and brought it down with as much power as he could muster.

Oracus teleported at the last second and got away from Gravaz. There was a roar of fury as Gravaz's flail missed its target, and Oracus took the spare seconds to aim a fireball at Lapsin and help Bandor escape from his jaws.

With the rain still falling, and with hundreds of Jowra's soldiers entering the city, Oracus had no choice but to try and kill Gravaz. With the Elephant Lavorian occupying the other three Riders in Tallarin, he was the only one who could stop Jowra's forces from taking control of this side of the city. He focused his power again, and threw one last fireball at the Ulatori who opposed him. Gravaz reacted quickly and threw a fireball of his own, and when the two collided in the air between them, there was an explosion that shook buildings all around.

Oracus hit the ground hard and felt pain shoot through his whole body. His ears were ringing, and he couldn't see much of what was going on near to him. The feeling was similar to that he had felt outside Fervia, when the fireball had exploded on Gravaz's chest. This time though, the force had been tenfold.

"Oracus? Oracus! Are you okay?" The voice sounded like a whisper at first. And then a face hovered over his own and the voice became louder. "Talk to me, Oracus!"

Oracus couldn't make out the face, everything was too much of a blur, but the person's hair was dark. It took him some time, but he finally recognised the voice. "I'm fine, Kivali," he grunted.

"I'm getting you out of here," she said.

"But what about Bandor?"

"Bandor's fine, don't worry."

There was a moment of darkness, and then Oracus noticed he was lying on softer ground. When he started to sit up, he saw he was inside a tiny room with a lot of straw on the floor and pails catching the water that leaked through the ceiling. Kivali was crouched next to him, and Bandor and Onca were there too.

"Where are we?" he asked.

"In a small hut near the palace," Kivali answered.

Oracus looked at Bandor and saw marks on his leg where Lapsin had bitten him. "You're hurt," he observed.

"I'm fine," Bandor assured. "It's just a graze."

"Is Gravaz dead?"

"No, but you gave him quite a shock again," Bandor said.

"The explosion shook half the city," Kivali added. "He's lucky to be alive. And so are you."

"We would have finished him off," Onca stated. "But Mammat and Zarad were quick to protect him and we only had time to get you out of there."

There was the bellow of what sounded like Mammat's trunk from a fair distance away.

"There were too many of them and they forced our men back," Kivali said with a shake of her head. "As soon as Mammat breached the wall a second time we were overrun."

"Then we need to get back out there," Oracus said firmly. He tried to push himself to his feet but wobbled and fell back down.

"You need to rest," Bandor told him. "You've taken a nasty whack to the head."

"But we can't let the enemy reach the families in the palace!"

"They're already using the secret passages to the mountains. They're safe."

"So we're just going to let Jowra's army win?" Oracus questioned, mortified.

"We're going to keep fighting for as long as we can, but their victory is inevitable. From the moment Mammat broke through the wall, this was only going to end one way."

"Then we need to defeat Mammat!" Oracus exclaimed. "When we get back out there, we focus on killing both Riders."

"Oracus, while you were fighting Gravaz, Zarad and Mammat were powerful enough to hold off three Riders and Lavorians," Kivali warned.

Oracus tried to stand for a second time, determined to

get back to the wall and fight, but his head started to spin and vomit rose to his throat. He sat back down, and that's when he heard her voice in his head.

"Alticon!" it pleaded. "Help me!"

Oracus's eyes widened in shock, and then an image of Catania flashed through his mind, her eyes as red as the blood on her hands.

"Alticon!" she screamed again. "Alticon, please!"

Twenty-Nine

Confronting A Demon

The sound of battle was getting louder. The clanging of swords was no longer confined to the wall, it was now spreading through Tallarin's streets and advancing towards the palace.

For the third time, Oracus tried to stand. This time, he managed to hold himself up, despite the dizziness creeping up on him again. But it wasn't just his head that was sore, he'd damaged his back while fighting Gravaz and now he was struggling to move.

"Oracus, sit back down!" Kivali ordered.

"But we can't stay here," Oracus argued. "I need to go to the palace and you all need to fight."

"What's going on?" Bandor said inside Oracus's head. *"I can sense your apprehension."*

"I just saw Catania again and she needs help."

"Then I'm coming with you," Bandor insisted.

"No, Bandor. Help them to fight and make sure Kivali stays safe. I can handle this alone." Oracus could sense Bandor was uncomfortable leaving him. *"Honestly, I'll be fine."* He turned his attention back to Kivali. "I can't fight, but it's

unfair to have two Riders and two Lavorians sat in a barn while Jowra's soldiers continue to slaughter ours."

"But I can't want to go anywhere without you," Kivali said.

"You can and you will!" Oracus forced. "Bandor will be with you and he'll tell you if I'm in trouble."

Kivali frowned but acquiesced. "Fine," she said. Then she wrapped her arms around Oracus in a farewell hug and he felt his heart lift. "I'll see you in the palace," she finished. With a final sorrowful look at Oracus, she led Onca and Bandor out the barn and out of sight.

When Oracus stumbled out the barn himself, he took a moment to gather his bearings and then followed the streets uphill towards the palace. By the time the palace was in sight, the pain in his back was beginning to overwhelm him and he dropped to his knees. He couldn't walk any further, and although the palace was no more than a short sprint away, it may as well have been on the other side of Pharia. It was so close – Catania was so close – but he was too weak to get there. He fell on his face on the wet streets of Tallarin, and when he finally blacked out, he travelled further away from the palace than he had ever been before.

*

The air that had once been fresh with the smell of cut grass and pine trees was replaced with an air full of smoke and death. The stench made a young Jowra heave.

King Amarad's forces had arrived in the small village of Emsbleek and Jowra had been ordered by his father to stay with his mother and sisters in their tiny wooden home.

"But I'm fifteen," Jowra had argued. "I can fight with you!"

"You're old enough to be the man of the house. And you need to keep the women safe if I don't come back." His father had held his shoulders with those rough but warm hands and fixed him with a challenging glare. Then he had embraced the girls and left with nothing but his pitchfork.

Jowra retched again. His father would likely never return. Emsbleek was a village of shopkeepers, not fighters, and King Amarad was ruthless and renowned for his relentless pursuit of power.

"Why is he attacking our village?" Jowra asked himself as he wiped vomit from his lips. "We aren't a threat."

The sobs of his mother brought Jowra to compose himself. He looked out the front of the house and saw an evening sky bright with the orange of fire, and black smoke rising in tendrils above the houses that were alight. The soldiers were getting nearer to them, and Jowra noted the closeness of the screams coming from villagers.

"We need to get out of here," Jowra said to his mother, turning to her and his younger sisters.

"Not without your father!"

Jowra approached the three of them and held them all tightly. "He isn't coming back."

"You don't know that," his mother denied.

Jowra kissed her cheek. He moved to the back of the house and checked that the street there was empty. Then he looked at his beautiful, innocent sisters; only four and six years old and being subjected to *this*. "If we face the soldiers then we'll be killed. If we hide in here then they'll burn the house down with us all still inside. But if we leave now then Lillia and Pip will be safe."

His mother looked at him helplessly.

"He told me to keep you safe and this is the only way I can," Jowra forced.

His mother stared at him a little longer, and then nodded. "We leave out the back?" she asked.

"There are no soldiers there," Jowra said with a nod. "If we cross the square then we can escape into the forest. Are you ready?"

Both Lillia and Pip had tears welling in their beautiful, innocent eyes, but they were brave enough to hold back their sobs. Jowra checked the back of the house a final time, and then led them and his mother onto the street.

"You need to keep really quiet," he whispered. He could feel his heart thumping inside his chest. "And make sure you find a place to hide if you see any soldiers."

They reached the square at the end of street without drawing any unwanted attention. The square was empty too, and the shops were all abandoned. Jowra stopped for a moment and focused his senses, listening for any soldiers who might be lurking nearby. All he could hear were the endless screams of the villagers who had already been caught.

"I think it's safe," he said. He could see the trees of the forest waiting patiently for them on the other side of the square. "Come on!"

But the moment they started crossing the square, several soldiers who had been surveying the square from inside the shops came to intercept them. "Seize them!"

Jowra didn't need to tell his mother or sisters to run.

Without a second's hesitation, they took off towards the trees, hoping the soldiers wouldn't be fast enough to catch them.

But their efforts were futile; the soldiers were far quicker than Lillia and Pip. And soon, all four of them had been wrestled to the ground.

Jowra kicked and punched with all his strength, but the soldiers were bigger than him and their numbers too great. Lillia and Pip's screams cut through him like a blade and he called their names to try and silence their fears.

"You told us we'd be safe!" his mother cried.

Jowra fought harder against the hands that held him and caught a soldier in the eye with his elbow. He managed to wriggle free, but there were still too many soldiers around his mother and sisters for him to save them all. He had no choice but to leave them, and he ran to the forest alone.

Two of the soldiers pursued Jowra to the treeline but they couldn't catch him. And once he was in the trees he knew how to hide himself. His unlikely escape drew angry shouts from the soldiers, but their shouts did nothing to drown out the petrified cries of Lillia and Pip.

In those trees surrounding Emsbleek, hiding from the soldiers who had almost caught him, Jowra made a promise to never rest until King Amarad was dead.

*

When Oracus came around, he was no longer on the cold, wet streets of Tallarin. Instead, he was being dragged through the workshop in the palace by several blue-skinned Sashtrams. When he groaned, the Sashtrams dropped him and gathered in a circle.

"We're taking you to safety, sir," one said.

"We saw you collapse out there," another added.

The pain in Oracus's body was still agonising, but the fury and guilt he'd felt while dreaming of Jowra somehow helped him to stand unaided. And his mind was now so alert he could sense Kivali's power even on the other side of the city.

"Thank you for helping me," he said to the Sashtrams. Then he teleported, and he landed on the long, winding staircase that led to Catania's quarters. He tried to climb, but his legs buckled and he fell onto his hands and knees.

The palace trembled around him, and the stone walls groaned in protest. Cracks appeared in the ceiling above, and dust fell all around. Suddenly, Oracus's vision flickered, and he could see Catania as if he was in the room with her. Her quarters were no longer pristine – there was blood on the white marble floor, with pieces of broken sculptures scattered everywhere. The window that overlooked the ocean had been smashed too, and there was a cold breeze circling the room. In the corner, Alticon was shackled to the wall.

"You remember our agreement, don't you, Catania?" a deep voice emanated from Catania's mouth like it was her own. "I would allow your precious Wolf to live if you surrendered your city to me."

Catania's eyes flashed from red to blue. "But it's not my fault!" she cried, her voice returning to its usual tone. "I haven't commanded my army to defend."

The demon inside Catania became impatient. The palace shook under the force of its mind and the breeze in the room built to a destructive cyclone. Shattered glass and broken marble rose into the air and orbited Catania's body, while Alticon whined in desperation from the corner.

"Your ineptitude sickens me!" the demon bellowed. "You have left me no choice."

"Please, no!"

Alticon howled in the seconds that followed, and Catania walked through the cyclone towards him. She pulled an elegant dagger from under her ragged white gown and the Wolf tried desperately to free himself. But the shackles held firm, and Catania's eyes were scarlet and mad. She stabbed Alticon three times in the chest and he quickly succumbed to his fate.

When Oracus regained control of his own body, he picked himself up and climbed the stairs as quickly as he could, ignoring the pain. He was confused and angry, and he was terrified of what he would find when he finally reached Catania, but he had no choice but to confront her.

The higher he climbed, the worse the damage to the palace became. When he reached the top of the staircase, he found the guard he had met on his first day in Tallarin lying dead. The magical sliding door had been ripped off its hinges too.

Oracus proceeded warily into Catania's quarters and stepped through the debris that littered the floor. The winds that had roared in his vision had now subsided, but the room was in ruin. The walls were cracked and crumbling, while the ceiling was beginning to cave in. On the other side of the room, Catania was knelt in a pool of blood, cradling Alticon's lifeless body.

"I couldn't stop it," she said hopelessly. Her face was wet

with tears. "He's controlling me."

Oracus approached her and her fiery eyes snapped up at him. He recoiled worriedly. "It's okay. We can make this better," he said.

"Nothing will make this better. He deserved a better life than I gave him." She put her face in Alticon's fur and sobbed.

"It wasn't your fault," Oracus tried.

"You know nothing," she denied. "Everything is my fault. This whole mess is my fault."

Oracus tried to approach her again, but the wind inside the room started to return.

"Stay away from me!" Catania yelled. "Don't come any closer."

"You can beat this, Catania," Oracus urged. "You don't have to give in to him."

"You have no idea how powerful he is," she claimed.

The winds built to a cyclone as powerful as the one that had destroyed the room. Catania dropped Alticon's body and moved away from him. The debris was lifted into a whirlwind that circled her, and the wind was so fierce that Oracus was forced to take a step backwards.

Catania came to the centre of the room with her red eyes glowing. She hovered above the ground, and lightning flickered at her fingertips as half the palace seemed to spin around her.

"The boy whose powers rival my own," she said in the voice of the King. There was an aura of supreme power about her now, like a dark shadow was shrouding her. "He stands before me for the first time, but he is alone and weak."

"Why aren't you here with your army?" Oracus said, keeping his voice as fearless as he could. "Are you a coward?"

Jowra returned a deep laugh that echoed off the walls. "I didn't need to be. The ease with which your city has fallen is proof of that."

"You haven't won yet!" Oracus shouted.

"Don't be so naïve," Jowra replied. "The wall is breached and your numbers are dwindling. It has taken very little effort."

"Then why are you still tormenting your own daughter? Does controlling her mind give you pleasure?"

"Conquering Tallarin isn't all I am using her for," Jowra claimed. "There is a certain *boy* in her city who interests me."

"You want *my* power because I'm a Vassath," Oracus said knowingly.

"Yes! Very good!" Jowra mocked. "But here is my dilemma: I could keep you in Melzor as my assistant and risk you trying to kill me, or I could kill you and take your power for myself."

"I would never join you anyway," Oracus made clear.

"Of that I have no doubt," Jowra said, appearing amused. "But please humour me with why…"

"Because you killed my father!"

"It wasn't *I* who killed your father. His death was an accident."

"And I'm sure Amarad would have said the same about your father, wouldn't he?" Oracus challenged cleverly.

The fire burned in Catania's eyes for a second. It seemed Jowra was taken by surprise. "Then you seek revenge?" he finally said. "Which means I have no choice but to kill you. And I must use Catania to do it. Does my controlling her mind make sense to you now?"

"You could have killed me yourself instead of sacrificing everyone else," Oracus said. "It makes you look scared."

Jowra cackled delightedly. "I'm the most powerful King there has ever been. I'm scared of nothing." The whirlwind inside the room expanded and debris cut at Oracus's skin. "Have you discovered how you and I are related yet, Oracus?" Jowra bellowed over the noise.

"You're my grandfather," Oracus replied with a sneer.

"Very good! So you know Catania is your mother?"

"I've known for a while," Oracus stated. "And I've come here to save her from you."

"There is only one way to rid me from her body," Jowra said heartlessly. "So now *you* are left with a dilemma: let me kill you and take your power, or kill your own mother."

The cyclone around Catania began to diminish. Oracus saw that her eyes were blue again, and she was crying. He tried to approach her, but she held up a hand to make him stop. "Please don't come any closer," she implored in her own soft voice. "He's right. There's only one way you can stop this."

"I'm not killing you!" Oracus yelled.

"Think of it as saving Pharia," she said.

"Killing you will not save Pharia! Nothing can save Pharia."

"You're wrong," she said with a shake of her head. "Pharia can be saved, but you need to be alive to do it."

Tears came to Oracus's eyes as he searched for a way to keep his mother alive. They had only just found each other, and now their reunion was to come to a premature end.

"I know this isn't fair on you, but it must be done. Kill me and then live to kill him."

"But I can save you!" Oracus protested.

Catania's eyes were full of hatred again, but her voice was still her own. "Do it now before it's too late," she begged.

"Yes, do it now before it's too late!" Jowra repeated.

The cyclone built to a phenomenal strength and the palace began to cave in on itself. Lightning between Catania's fingers was crackling angrily, and her head tilted back as Jowra summoned all his power. Oracus had no choice but to pull the bow from his back. When he nocked the arrow, he hesitated for a moment, and then fired it into the wind.

The debris dropped to the floor and the roaring winds fell to silence as the arrow pierced Catania's chest. Her body hit the floor beside Alticon, and Oracus clambered over the rubble to get to her.

Catania's eyes were on his when he crouched over her body. They were like the sky on a warm summer's day. She had a smile on her face, and she lifted a hand to touch his cheek.

"You did well," she said. "He's gone."

He wished he could, but Oracus couldn't find the words. He wanted to comfort his mother, to tell her everything would be okay, but his throat tightened and stopped him from speaking. He was looking down at the woman he had wanted to meet his whole life. Yet all the questions he wanted to ask her were going to pass unanswered.

Catania coughed as the final seconds came. Her hand

dropped away from Oracus's face and her smile vanished. She gasped for air, and then uttered her final words, "I never stopped thinking about you."

Her beautiful eyes closed, and Oracus was left alone.

Thirty

Past And Present

Frost sparkled like crystals on the fine spring grass. It was early morning and the sun had barely risen above the rooftops. There was still a chill in the air that nibbled Catania's fingertips.

The streets of Melzor were empty at such a time, and Catania skipped and hummed happily. She was heading for the farmyard to see Padaquin, the farmer's son. He was handsome and charming and *older,* so she made the trip as often as she could. But such escapades she had to keep a secret, because if her father found out, Padaquin would likely be killed.

Catania was eighteen years old, and Padaquin twenty-two. His age was what attracted Catania to him most, she thought. Or perhaps it was his chiselled muscles and gruff voice. Or maybe his green eyes. Whatever it was, his company made her happy. It was such a pleasant change from being in the presence of her father.

"Good morning," she said shyly from the doorway of the barn.

Padaquin looked up from the cow he was milking. "Back

again?" he said. "You must be trying to get me in trouble."

"I'm not," she said quickly. "I just wanted to see you."

Padaquin smiled despite himself, and Catania took that as her cue to enter.

"Have you been here long?" she asked.

"Couple of hours," Padaquin answered, back to milking.

"Can I help you with anything?"

"You can feed the chickens," he suggested.

Catania stepped carefully across the barn and sprinkled a handful of grain into the chicken coop. Then she tiptoed back.

Padaquin laughed. "Task completed like a palace girl."

"What's that supposed to mean?"

"You're far too worried about getting your shoes dirty," he teased.

"If I go home covered in muck then my father will know where I've been," she argued. "And I doubt that would end well for you."

Padaquin's eyes twinkled like gemstones, like they always did when he made her mad. Catching sight of them made her heart flutter.

"So where does he think you are today?" Padaquin asked.

"He doesn't think I'm anywhere," Catania replied. "He's with his Dragons. Probably hatching a cunning plan of some sort."

"Time that would be better spent providing for the people in his city."

"You don't think he provides for his people?" Catania asked.

"He lives comfortably in his palace while my father and I

have barely enough coin to buy grain for the chickens."

"You wouldn't leave Melzor though, would you? So it can't be *that* bad."

"I would leave if I had the money," Padaquin answered seriously.

"Well I have money," Catania said, surprising herself with what she was insinuating.

Padaquin looked quizzically at her. "Are you suggesting we run away together?"

Catania blushed a deep red. "What if I am?"

"I'm not sure that would be a good idea."

"Why not?"

"Because if you disappeared then every soldier in Pharia would be sent to search for you," Padaquin said. "We would always be looking over our shoulder."

"But you would consider it?"

Padaquin fixed her with a serious glare and then turned his back to feed the pigs.

"I'll take that as a yes," she said, a huge smile spreading across her face.

*

Oracus stood over Catania and Alticon's dead bodies, their blood merging and beginning to flow through the rubble. It was another ache in Oracus's heart that could be added to all the others, seeing his mother dead. But at least she was at peace now, and no longer being tormented by the secrets she was keeping.

Oracus wiped the tears from his cheeks when the damaged ceiling above him creaked. If he could have stayed alone with the bodies a while longer, he would have, but he needed to get them out before the room caved under the weight of the mountain.

"How do you think the people of Tallarin will react to this?" a voice asked from the doorway.

Oracus looked up to see Quent watching him. He sighed gratefully. "I never thought I'd be glad to see you," he said. "Help me get these bodies out before the ceiling collapses."

Quent shook his head and smiled. "I don't think I can help you with that."

"If you don't then their bodies will be buried here," Oracus protested.

"That's a shame," Quent said. "But if I die trying to get them out, nobody will know what really happened here. And I think it's important the surviving people of Tallarin know you killed their Princess!"

"No, Quent, I had to," Oracus said. "Did you not see Jowra controlling her?"

"What I saw was Princess Catania pleading for her life, and instead of sparing her, you shot her with an arrow. And poor Alticon was just collateral damage."

"You can't be serious?" Oracus said in desperation.

"If you live beyond today, you could deny it. But would they believe me or the Vassath Rider who is powerful enough to destroy half the palace?"

Oracus stood with his mouth open. If he hadn't been in pain or stuck behind a mound of debris, he would have killed Quent with his bare hands.

"I did try to stop you, but you were far too strong for me," he continued, tapping the doorframe nonchalantly with a finger. "Somehow, I managed to escape, but there was no way of me recovering Catania or Alticon's bodies."

"You liar!" Oracus shouted. He grabbed his bow, but before he could nock an arrow to the string, Quent was gone.

"Bandor, the ceiling is falling in Catania's quarters," Oracus said worriedly in his mind. *"Where are you?"*

"I'm coming for you," came the reply. *"I'm running up the palace steps."*

The walls were crumbling now and the floor was beginning to lurch dangerously. Oracus felt his heart thumping inside him and he wondered if he could even get himself out, let alone Catania and Alticon.

"I'm going to be buried in here, Bandor. I'm stuck!"

The ceiling creaked again and more rubble fell into the room. Oracus backed away, but a lump of rock caught his head and knocked him to the floor.

"Hurry, Bandor," were the words that left his lips. "Hurry."

*

Four years passed by and Catania still skipped through Melzor's streets to see Padaquin most mornings. She was no longer the naïve girl she had been before, but that didn't stop her loving the farmer's boy more than ever.

Their regular trysts on the farmyard were still a risk, but Catania hadn't once been caught by her father, so naturally she visited the farm more and more. If her father hadn't noticed her disappearances thus far, he was never going to. He obviously had more pressing issues to concern himself with; like the *rebellion*.

It was spring again, and frosty too. But Catania didn't mind the cold, just as she no longer minded the dirt. These days, she helped Padaquin work through the mornings; she milked the cows, fed the pigs and chickens, mucked out the stables – she would often tell Padaquin she was a farmer's girl with a fine taste in clothes. Padaquin would often roll his eyes.

"Can you remember when we joked about running away from Melzor together?" Catania said as Padaquin rolled a bail of hay into the stable. "Do you think we would have coped on our own?"

"I think we would have been found. You would be back in the palace, most likely, and I would be dead."

Catania continued brushing the horse she was grooming. "Nobody would find us if we hid in the forest."

"Maybe," Padaquin said with a shrug.

Catania turned to face Padaquin and leaned against the horse. "I have something important to tell you," she said.

Padaquin's green eyes were instantly on her. "What is it?"

Catania put a delicate hand on her belly and smiled. "We've made a little person."

It took a while for the words to sink in, but when they did, Padaquin's face lit up like a firework.

"You're happy?" Catania asked him.

"Of course I'm happy!" he exclaimed. But his ecstasy quickly became an expression of uncertainty. "But what are we going to do?"

Catania looked seriously at him. "What would you say now if I suggested running away?"

It took Padaquin less than a second to answer. "I would say yes."

"You'd risk your life to be with me?"

"I would do anything for you, Catania," he said. "And we can't stay here now. The one thing we can't keep a secret is a baby."

Catania ran over to Padaquin and wrapped her arms around him. She laughed, and then she began to cry. "When should we go?" she asked between sobs.

"As soon as it's safe to," he answered.

*

"Oracus, wake up. I need help here!"

Oracus heard Bandor's voice inside his head when he came around, but it was the pain in his wrist that had brought him back to consciousness. When he opened his eyes, he saw the Lion's metal jaws were clamped tightly around his arm, teeth digging deep into the flesh, as he tried to wrestle him free of the rubble. Oracus wriggled and adjusted, and eventually his legs came loose.

"It's lucky only your legs were trapped," Bandor said. *"What happened up here?"*

"Did you see Quent on your way through the palace?" Oracus asked, ignoring Bandor's question.

"He was running through the workshop, screaming," Bandor answered. *"Why?"*

"Because he's going to tell everyone I killed Catania."

Bandor looked at Catania and Alticon's dead bodies and then glanced around the destroyed room. *"Tell me what happened!"*

"Jowra was controlling Catania and destroying the palace through her body. He made her kill Alticon and he tried to kill

me."

"So you killed her instead?"

"Bandor, I had no choice," Oracus insisted. *"But Quent saw it all and he's going to make me sound like the villain."*

"Then we need to go after him!" Bandor ordered.

"I can barely walk. My back and legs hurt so much," Oracus said.

"Then I'll carry you, you just need to climb on my–" Bandor paused and his ears twitched towards the door. *"There's someone coming."*

"Someone to help get us out?" Oracus said hopefully.

"Oracus, I don't think it's someone who wants to help..."

Oracus was instantly paralysed with fear. He and Bandor stared at the door and waited to be found by their enemy. Whoever this person was, their heavy boots were like an approaching battledrum with every step, distant and quiet at first, but more thunderous with every beat.

"There was nowhere you could hide from me!" a deep voice growled from outside the door.

Next moment, Gravaz was stooping through the doorway, his huge frame filling what was left of the destroyed room. He carried no weapon and Lapsin wasn't by his side, but the sight of him still filled Oracus with terror.

"Tallarin has been defeated," Gravaz said triumphantly. His scarred face twisted into a smile and he rubbed his enormous grey hands together. "Your death is all that remains."

Oracus watched from the floor as Gravaz climbed slowly over the rubble that separated them. Bandor growled at Oracus's side but the Ulatori was unfazed by the warning.

When he was just feet from Oracus, he removed his eye-patch and unfastened his chestplate to reveal a misty eye and more scarring across his upper torso.

"Look at what you did to me!" Gravaz shouted angrily. Oracus flinched and shuffled backwards. "Stand up so I can kill you properly."

Bandor took a step forwards to protect Oracus. Gravaz snarled and his one yellow eye glowered at them both.

"I can't stand," Oracus said.

"Then I'll force you to," Gravaz responded.

Bandor roared in defiance. He leaped at Gravaz to knock him down, but the Ulatori caught the Lion's head in his hands and threw him across the room. More of the ceiling fell when Bandor landed, and Oracus shielded his eyes from the dust.

"Even your Lavorian cannot save you," Gravaz said as he grabbed Oracus by the hair and lifted him to his feet.

Oracus screamed in pain, then Gravaz struck him in the stomach and let him fall back to the floor.

"Would you like this to end quickly?" Gravaz asked. "Or very, very slowly?"

Another growl came from where Gravaz had thrown Bandor. The Lavorian climbed free of the debris that had landed on him and he attacked the Ulatori for a second time. Gravaz tried to dodge Bandor, but a claw tore the skin of his arm. When Bandor landed next to Oracus, Gravaz aimed a ball of fire at their feet.

Oracus gasped before the explosion came, and he noticed the look of victory on Gravaz's face too. The force of the blast lifted Oracus off the ground, and the heat that immersed his skin was intense and agonising. He was thrown backwards through the broken window of Catania's quarters, and then he was falling towards the ocean far below.

*

Padaquin and Catania left Melzor and travelled across desert towards the safety of the forest. When they reached the trees, they spent several weeks sleeping on piles of leaves and rationing their dwindling supply of food. Then eventually, they found an abandoned village that would provide them with shelter.

The village appeared to have been ravaged by fire. But over the many years that had passed by since, moss and ivy had almost entirely consumed it. There was a sign in the village; *Emsbleek*, it read. And there was a river nearby too, which provided Padaquin and Catania with fresh water.

For a whole year, the two of them stayed alone in Emsbleek, in a tiny house that had avoided the fire. The house had a bed and a stove, luxuries they had not expected before fleeing Melzor, and it had a roof that sheltered them from the rain too. Padaquin learned to hunt game with a makeshift bow, while Catania would pick fruits from the bushes around the village. And in time, their beautiful baby boy arrived, with blonde hair like Catania's and emerald green eyes like Padaquin's. He was a Prince of Melzor, and a handsome young boy too. But he was a Prince who would never take the throne, for his parents were now enemies of the King, particularly his peasant father.

The whole time they were in the forest, they lived in constant fear of being caught. Not a day went by when they didn't say how much they loved each other. Then eventually, the day they dreaded most finally came.

"They must have seen the smoke of our fire!" Catania gasped as the sound of a horn bellowed from within the trees surrounding Emsbleek. "You need to leave now, Padaquin. And take Oracus with you!"

"There's no way I'm leaving you here," Padaquin retorted.

"We don't have a choice. There's no other way."

"If you take Oracus then I'll be the one to stay behind and get caught."

"You know that won't work. He'll never stop searching for me unless he finds me. I'll tell him you died, and he never needs to know about Oracus."

"But he'll kill you," Padaquin stated.

"He won't kill me. He'll just keep me in the palace until he thinks he can trust me again," Catania said. "And when he let's me out, I'll come and find you."

There was a rustle of leaves from the bushes nearby that startled them both.

"Go now before they see you," Catania urged. "Go!"

Padaquin gazed into Catania's eyes one last time before he left. Then he scooped up Oracus and headed for the trees that would take him further north.

He didn't know it, but that was the last time Padaquin would see the mother of his son.

Thirty-One

The Black Forest

Oracus came around to salty water lapping his face. When he opened his eyes, he realised he was floating on the ocean, face down beside Bandor on Catania's broken dresser.

The memories from the palace all came back to him at once – Catania killing Alticon, Jowra almost destroying the palace… himself firing an arrow into his mother's chest. He looked around for the palace but could see nothing except a few mountains in the distance with stormclouds churning above.

"How long have I been out?" he asked Bandor.

"An hour or so," his Lion's voice purred back at him. *"I was worried about you."*

"I'm fine," Oracus said. *"But my body is sore."*

Oracus looked down at himself and saw blood was seeping from the wound on his arm that Gravaz had dealt him. He felt pain in his back too, and in his legs where he had been trapped under rubble. He fidgeted to find comfort, but only succeeded in splashing himself with water.

"Do you think they managed to hold the city?" Oracus said hopefully.

"I think it was already defeated before we left," Bandor admitted.

"Then do you think everyone got out safely?"

"I'm sure all the women and children are already in the mountains," Bandor said. *"But I don't know where they will go."*

"To Afarra probably," Oracus answered.

"The other side of Pharia. It'll be a miracle if Jowra's soldiers don't intercept them on the way."

A feeling of dread crept over Oracus's body. Thousands of innocent people would be captured by Jowra because he and the other Riders had failed to defend Tallarin. And thousands of soldiers had already lost their lives because he hadn't been able to protect them.

"I hope Kivali is with those who escaped," he said.

"She was still alive when I came to help you. She's tough, it'll take a lot to kill her. And she won't let anyone come to harm."

"I should be with her," Oracus said. *"She'll need help."*

"It isn't worth worrying about," Bandor said. *"There's nothing you can do. We're adrift in the middle of the ocean and nobody is looking for us."*

"Then we need to get back to land. We should swim back to Tallarin."

"The current has carried us all this way in an hour, Oracus. We'd never make it. And you're injured too."

"Then do we just drift until we die?"

"Maybe. But we're heading west," Bandor stated. *"There's a chance we'll reach land eventually."*

"But there's more of a chance we won't."

Oracus's thoughts turned to Garrin and Afarra, and whether his friend knew Tallarin had fallen. What would Torvanon do when the news reached them – send his army to Melzor, or set up a defence and hope to survive?

"Do you think Jowra has other forces spare that he didn't send to Tallarin?" he asked Bandor.

"Are you wondering if he'll need to regroup before attacking Afarra?" Bandor enquired.

"I guess so," Oracus admitted. *"I hate the thought of Jowra taking control so swiftly. If we do make it back to land alive, I'd like to reach Afarra before all my friends are dead."*

"There's no guarantee Jowra would defeat Afarra if he did attack," Bandor said.

"Did you see the way Mammat broke down the wall at Tallarin?" Oracus replied. *"He would step over Afarra's wall and trample the buildings to dust."*

"But Torvanon is in Afarra. He's a different proposition to the Riders Mammat faced in Tallarin."

Oracus sighed deeply, and then laughed. *"We talk of this like we've known it all our lives. It wasn't so long ago that Garrin and I knew nothing of the land beyond Thessley. Now we're losing a war we don't truly understand."*

"The war isn't lost yet," Bandor argued. He shook his head and water flicked off his mane.

"Tallarin is Jowra's, the rebellion has been halved, and we're stuck out here without any way of getting home. I'd consider that losing."

"Yes, Tallarin is defeated. And yes, the rebellion has taken a hit. But actually, I can see land over there."

Oracus's head snapped around and he peered towards where Bandor was looking. Sure enough, the once-endless horizon to the north-west was now disrupted by what he perceived to be a large group of black trees. A grin crossed his face, and then he patted Bandor affectionately on his head. *"We're not dead yet!"* he exclaimed.

The flow of the ocean carried them towards land, and before long, they were fast approaching a pebbled shoreline hidden under a thin blanket of snow. A thick mist now hovered around them, and the water had turned icy cold. Oracus shivered whenever the waves licked his skin.

When the wooden dresser ran ashore, Oracus scraped his knees on the stones and groaned. He crawled up the beach alongside Bandor, trying to distance himself from the water he had been sure would kill him.

"Now that's over, we just need to decide if we should go around or through," Bandor said.

"Around or through what?" Oracus asked. But when he looked up, he saw what Bandor meant. They were faced by a forest of black trees that looked imposing in its magnificence.

"If we go through, maybe the trees will protect you from the cold," Bandor suggested.

Oracus shuddered and crossed his arms to keep himself warm. *"Good idea."*

"Can you stand?"

Oracus shook his head. *"You're going to have to carry me."* He pulled himself onto Bandor's back and rested his head on his Lion's mane. *"I wish I could walk. Maybe then the cold wouldn't feel so bitter."*

The shore was desolate in both directions for as far as the mist would allow them to see. It was quiet too, except for the lapping of waves on the pebbles. But when they stepped into the forest, an eerie silence enveloped them and all became dark.

Oracus tightened his grip around Bandor's neck as the Lavorian crept cautiously through the trees. It was a forest unlike that which Oracus was familiar with; he would never have enjoyed hunting game in here. It was too still and haunting. He was glad he had Bandor to guide him, because alone he would never have found his way through.

For a time, Oracus used Bandor's senses to observe his surroundings. Deep undergrowth shrouded the forest floor, while low-hanging branches covered with spikes reached for his face as Bandor advanced ever faster. Eventually though, Oracus succumbed to sleep as exhaustion overwhelmed him.

When he woke up, what may have been several hours had passed by. The darkness of the forest still lingered, but Bandor had come to a halt and his nose was pressed to the ground.

"What is it?" Oracus asked sleepily.

"I can smell something," Bandor replied uneasily.

"Smell what?"

"I don't know."

"Is it a village?"

"No. Someone has been here," he said, *"A creature of some kind. I recognise the scent."*

Oracus tapped into Bandor's senses again to try and help but couldn't identify the smell. *"I don't know what it is either,"* he said.

Bandor sniffed some more, lifted his head and stepped forwards. Then the ground around them swallowed them up.

It took Oracus a moment to realise he was hanging in a net above the forest floor. He had screamed at first, and now he was cursing at the pain he felt in his injured legs and back. *"What is this?"* he shouted.

"It's a trap!" Bandor answered. And he immediately scratched at the netting with his claws.

When the netting ripped, Oracus and Bandor fell with a thud and Oracus screamed again. There was a rustle from a bush nearby, and Oracus had no more time to consider the pain he was in.

"It is a Human!" a deep voice bellowed from somewhere in the darkness.

Oracus's eyes were wide with panic, and Bandor stood over him protectively.

"Sarvon will be happy and Valaroth will celebrate!" another voice boomed. And there were several approvals called out by more voices.

"Do it, Danzig," the first voice ordered impatiently.

There was a hiss in the air prior to a tiny dart striking Oracus's neck. For a second, he was relieved of all his pain. Then he was struck by dizziness and the darkness of the forest intensified.

Thirty-Two

Accept Or Die

Oracus sat with his mother and father in their home in Thessley, talking in front of the fire. The warmth of the flames was blissful, but not so much as the love he felt when the three of them were together. Oracus's heart fluttered joyously; a family who made him feel happy and safe was what he'd desired above all else, and he would cherish the feeling like no other.

But there was something missing in their cosy, thatched house – it was a presence in his mind he had become very accustomed to recently. Bandor.

There was a moment of regret as Oracus realised he would have to let Bandor go. It was a shame, but he had his family with him now, and all was peaceful. He closed his eyes and soaked up the joy.

Then there was a sharp knock at the door.

"That'll be Broid," his father advised, lifting himself from his chair.

The knock sounded again, loud and impatient this time.

"Okay, okay. I'm coming!" Padaquin shouted.

A loud crash thundered through the house as the door

was kicked off its hinges. Gravaz stood imperious in the doorway with Lapsin by his side.

"Who are you?" Oracus's father demanded.

Gravaz stooped through the doorway and struck Padaquin's face with his fist. "I am Gravaz, trusted servant of King Jowra."

Catania screamed and Oracus jumped from his seat. He tried to link his mind with Bandor's and summon his power but realised he was no longer a Rider.

Gravaz laughed sadistically. "Men usually kneel when I enter a room," he said arrogantly.

"I will never kneel to you!" Oracus refused. He faced the Ulatori bravely, but Gravaz's fist met his stomach and his legs buckled.

"That's better," Gravaz said as Oracus dropped to his knees. "Now you will accompany me to Melzor. You can watch your mother and father being fed to Wravias and Pseubas in the keep–"

Icy water splashed over Oracus's face and wrenched him from his dream of Gravaz and his parents. A distressing mixture of relief and pain coursed through his body.

His hands were bound above his head and he hung several feet in the air from a frame in a small village square. Snow and frost covered the rooftops of surrounding wooden buildings, and the icy air gnawed at his bare skin. He had been stripped of his clothes and his weapons had been taken from him too. He was alone and vulnerable on the square, but a hundred yellow eyes were staring at him from all around. Powerful men and women wearing long, fur robes were everywhere. They were Ulatoris, just like Gravaz, all several feet taller than Oracus with the same grey skin. Even in his drowsy state, the sight of the Ulatoris made Oracus try to free himself. He yanked at the vines binding his wrists, but to no avail.

"State your business here, Rider!" An Ulatori with an ugly crown on his head stomped across the square. He was colossal, even compared to the other Ulatoris, and he towered over Oracus. He was bare-chested, despite the temperature, and his muscular torso was half covered in tattoos. "STATE YOUR BUSINESS HERE!" he bellowed again, spraying spittle from his huge mouth.

"I don't know where I am," Oracus said fearfully.

The Ulatori growled loudly and the crowd to his rear growled with him. Some of them jeered and waved their hands unhappily.

"You are in Valaroth, Human. Home of the Ulatoris. Now tell me why you are here before I kill you."

"I'm here by mistake," Oracus said. "I didn't mean to intrude." He searched for Bandor's mind but felt nothing. His fear increased tenfold.

"You meant not to *intrude*?" the Ulatori returned. "Do not insult my intelligence, Rider!" He struck Oracus's face with his giant fist and Oracus whimpered in pain. "Do you know who I am?"

Oracus shook his head. "I don't."

"I am Sarvon, leader of Valaroth and protector of the Black Forest. If anyone trespasses on my domain, they will be killed. There are no exceptions."

"Please," Oracus begged. "I really didn't mean to be in your forest. I had no other choice."

Sarvon waved his hand dismissively. "Bring the Lavorian," he ordered.

The screech of something huge was heard overhead, and

a creature descended from the sky. It landed softly in the square and folded its wings into its body, then it screeched again. The beast was a Lavorian – Oracus knew so because of the armour covering its body – but the animal it resembled he had never seen before. It stood on six legs and had sharp spines from the crown of its head to the tip of its long tail. It stood taller than any of the Ulatoris and its green eyes were narrow and fierce above a snout dripping with drool. Now the Lavorian's wings were folded, it appeared not to have any at all.

When the Lavorian approached Oracus and Sarvon, Oracus noticed something limp in its mouth.

"Bandor!" he cried out. There was no reply from his Lavorian and Oracus feared the worst. "What have you done to him?"

Sarvon struck Oracus's face again. "He's not dead yet, but he will be. As will you."

The Lavorian dropped Bandor onto the ground in front of Oracus. The Lion didn't move.

"Are you going to tell me now why you are here?" Sarvon said.

"I'm not here intentionally, I promise! There was a battle–"

"There are always battles between Humans." Sarvon clasped Oracus's midriff in a huge hand. "A race so weak it fights and destroys anything it can in an attempt to prove its power."

Oracus nodded. "You're right!" he claimed. "But I don't want to fight. I want everything to be peaceful."

"Who won this battle you speak of?" Sarvon asked.

"Jowra, I think," Oracus answered. "Tallarin has been

defeated by him."

The crowd that gathered around the square hissed at the mention of Jowra's name and Sarvon began to crush Oracus in his hand. His lip snarled angrily and Oracus yelled out.

"Because you have conquered another city, you think you can conquer us?" Sarvon questioned fiercely.

"No!"

"Because you are strong enough to defeat others in your feeble race, you think you can overthrow us Ulatoris?"

"No!"

"It is a shame to kill a Rider and Lavorian, but your presence here leaves me no choice." Sarvon pulled a large axe from behind his back and the crowd of Ulatoris cheered and whistled. "Goodbye, Rider of Melzor." He lifted the axe above his head.

"Wait!" Oracus shouted. "I'm not a Rider of Melzor. I want Jowra dead!"

Oracus was sure his pleads would go unheard, but Sarvon didn't bring the axe down. Then the Ulatori's expression eased and he lowered his weapon.

"I will give you one minute to explain yourself," he said.

Hope flowed through Oracus. "There's a rebellion trying to kill Jowra. He forced me to leave my home, and he killed my mother and father!"

The Ulatoris nearby were hissing again. They wanted Oracus to be killed.

"I promise I'm not lying!" he yelled.

"How did you get into my forest?" Sarvon enquired.

"Jowra invaded Tallarin, where I was living, and I was forced to flee. Another Rider threw me into the ocean – he was an Ulatori called Gravaz!"

The name drew jeers from the Ulatoris. Some of the women screamed.

"Gravaz?" Sarvon bellowed. "He is a traitor!"

"When he threw me into the ocean, the tide brought me to your forest. Because of my injuries, I could do nothing but let my Lavorian carry me through the trees."

Sarvon turned away from Oracus and patted his own Lavorian on the side. Oracus had the feeling they were communicating in their minds.

"Your injuries are indeed quite severe," Sarvon said. "But we have the medicine here to help you recover."

"You want to keep me alive?" Oracus said with surprise.

"Only if you promise me something in return..."

"What could you possibly want from *me*?" Oracus asked.

"I want Gravaz!" Sarvon growled.

"You want me to kill him?"

"No." Sarvon shook his huge head. "I want you to bring him here."

"And you would trust me to leave and then come back?"

"I am no fool, Rider. I will keep you here until I am sure you are capable and willing to fulfil our agreement."

"And what if you decide I'm not?"

"Then I will just kill you as I was going to when you first arrived."

Oracus looked down at Bandor and realised he had no choice but to agree. "If it spares mine and my Lavorian's lives then I'll do whatever you ask."

Sarvon bowed his head in acknowledgment. He turned to the crowd of Ulatoris. "Cut him loose and take him to Shurgda."

The vines were cut and Oracus landed heavily in the

snow. He groaned, and two muscular Ulatoris dragged him to his feet with rough hands.

Oracus gasped as the pain in his body peaked again. Then he went limp and let them carry him across the square. "I guess this isn't the end of the journey," he said to himself under his breath.

Thank you so much for reading Fire Rider. I am so grateful for you getting this far!

As an indie-author, I rely on readers and their support so I can keep on producing books of high quality. That makes YOU a really important part of my journey.

To help me, please take a moment to add a review. It will honestly mean the world to me. And if you enjoyed the book, I would appreciate it if you could recommend it to anyone you know who may also enjoy it.

It has been my pleasure having you here!

Printed in Great Britain
by Amazon

74455858R00182